We're all carrying something—scars, stories, silence. This book reminds us that God doesn't waste pain. He redeems it. Derwin gives language to what we've buried and points us to real healing in Christ.

LECRAE, four-time Grammy Award winner and twelve-time Dove Award winner

In his biblical and compassionate way, my friend Derwin has written a powerful guide for those who have been carrying the weight of life's wounds and have decided it's time to heal. Truth and wisdom are the heartbeat of this book, which will guide you toward the wholeness you've been waiting for. If you're ready for your story to be redeemed for the Kingdom, read this book.

LYSA TERKEURST, #1 *New York Times* bestselling author and president of Proverbs 31 Ministries

It's Time to Heal is one of the most honest, compassionate, and spiritually grounded books on healing I've read in a long time. Derwin beautifully integrates faith, emotional honesty, trauma awareness, and even modern neuroscience in a way that feels deeply human and deeply hopeful. As a physician who has spent decades studying the brain, trauma, and recovery, I appreciate how clearly this book affirms what science and Scripture both teach: What we name we can heal; what we hide keeps hurting us. If you've been wounded—by life, by others, or by your own choices—and you're tired of surviving instead of living, this book will meet you with grace, courage, and truth. It doesn't shame you for your scars; it shows you how God can redeem them. I highly recommend this book to anyone who wants real healing, not just relief.

DANIEL G. AMEN, MD, founder of Amen Clinics and author of *Change Your Brain, Change Your Pain*

Many of us have learned to live with our wounds instead of letting Jesus heal them. In his new book, *It's Time to Heal*, Dr. Derwin L. Gray confronts the unresolved pain, shame, and trauma that too many believers try to carry alone. With pastoral warmth, theological depth, and courageous honesty, Derwin offers a biblically rich and deeply compassionate path for turning wounds into testimonies. This is not a shallow call to "move on" but a Spirit-led invitation to real, lasting wholeness. This powerful and hope-filled book will serve as a trusted guide for anyone ready to step out of shame and into the healing embrace of Jesus.

CRAIG GROESCHEL, senior pastor of Life.Church and *New York Times* bestselling author

Dr. Derwin Gray brings the rigor of a New Testament scholar and the raw testimony of a man who has been in the pit. Without pretense, and with hard-won faith, *It's Time to Heal* does honest, rare work, offering truth that is academically grounded, pastorally tender, and viscerally alive. Your wounds get to meet the healing of the God who does not run from your scars—because he still carries his own.

ANN VOSKAMP, *New York Times* bestselling author of *One Thousand Gifts* and *WayMaker*

It's Time to Heal is *exceptional*, and it's the essential book for our generation in this pivotal moment. Derwin presents practical steps for embracing the freedom available to all who are in Christ. Through his compelling writing, he transforms profound theological truths into accessible guidance, infused with pastoral compassion and prophetic insight. The powerful message that what Jesus has done for us far outweighs anything that has been done to us is the hope our world desperately needs. This is a truth that we, as followers of Jesus, can boldly embody and live out loud.

CHRISTINE CAINE, founder of A21 and Propel Women

Healing from our wounds can feel so complicated. But it doesn't have to be. My dear friend and one of the most trusted pastoral voices of our time, Dr. Derwin Gray, has written a gracious guide unpacking what God's Word actually says about our deepest pains and tenderly showing us a path forward because of the healing work of Jesus. I'm so thankful for these freeing pages! I'll be getting copies for many people I know.

HOSANNA WONG, international speaker and bestselling author of *Uncomplicate It* and *You Are More Than You've Been Told*

Derwin is a dear friend and a trusted voice, and he has written another powerful book. In *It's Time to Heal,* he offers practical, grace-filled guidance for anyone carrying hidden pain. Derwin reminds us that we don't have to hide our wounds and that real healing is possible. Drawing on the love of God and insights from neuroscience, he shows how deep, lasting healing can take place. With the heart of a pastor and the wisdom of a seasoned leader, he guides readers beyond the pain of the past and into the life God has for them. This book will help you get there.

BOB GOFF, four-time *New York Times* bestselling author

I've had the privilege of knowing Derwin Gray for years, and the best part is that he keeps growing in grace, transparency, and love. This book is an honest account of the grace of God meeting Derwin and many others just as they are. The world (and the church) needs more of this.

CAREY NIEUWHOF, bestselling author, podcaster, and speaker

With kindness, clarity, wisdom, and focus, *It's Time to Heal* offers an important path on the vital journey of pursuing health in body, soul, and spirit.

ANNIE F. DOWNS, *New York Times* bestselling author of *That Sounds Fun*

It's Time to Heal compassionately bridges clinical wisdom and gospel truth. With clarity and grace, Dr. Gray exposes the lies that exhaust the soul and invites readers into rest, self-advocacy, forgiveness, and true identity in Christ. This book is a trustworthy guide for anyone seeking deep, lasting healing.

DR. VICKEY MACLIN, PsyD, LPA, licensed psychological associate and associate director of graduate programs in counseling at Gordon-Conwell Theological Seminary

It's Time to Heal is a deeply thoughtful and beautifully integrated work. Derwin Gray brings together a clear and faithful biblical foundation with solid psychology and neurobiology, therapeutic wisdom, and spiritual formation insight in a way that is both accessible and profoundly helpful. This book does not offer shallow fixes or spiritual clichés. It's a needed resource for anyone who has experienced trauma, loss, or deep emotional wounds and for pastors, counselors, and leaders who walk with people on the long road toward healing. I highly recommend *It's Time to Heal.*

JIM CRESS, MA, LPC, CSAT, CMAT, cohost of the *Therapy & Theology* podcast, executive advisory board member for the American Association of Christian Counselors, and licensed professional counselor

In *It's Time to Heal*, Derwin L. Gray offers more than inspiration. He offers a pathway. This is a beautiful, practical, hope-filled guide for anyone carrying wounds. As a neurosurgeon, I have spent decades in the operating room repairing brains shattered by trauma, tumors, and tragedy. But I have learned that the deepest wounds are not always visible on a scan. They linger in the hidden places of the mind and heart. Derwin leads readers into that sacred space where real healing begins. His *HEAL* framework is clear, biblical, and deeply personal. As a man who has known the scars of war and the devastating loss of a son, I found this message healing my own wounds. Derwin seamlessly blends theology and neuroscience, showing you how to turn regret into resilience and pain into purpose. This is not a book you simply read. It is a book that walks with you toward wellness. If you long for lasting healing, this book will meet you there.

W. LEE WARREN, MD, neurosurgeon and author of *The Life-Changing Art of Self–Brain Surgery*

We all carry things we'd rather not look at. And most of the time, we either try to outrun them or spiritualize them. Derwin doesn't let you do either. This book is an honest invitation to face what happened to you and let Jesus meet you there. No shame, no clichés. Just real healing at the heart level. Derwin writes as a pastor who has done his own work. He understands that healing isn't soft. It takes courage. It takes humility. And most of all, it's worth it. If you're ready to stop pretending and to start becoming whole, this book is a wise guide for the journey.

TREY TUCKER, licensed therapist and author of *Tough Enough*

We live in a profoundly fractured world, carrying trauma and hidden wounds that we too often try to spiritualize away. In *It's Time to Heal*, my brother Dr. Derwin L. Gray offers a gritty, grace-saturated road map out of the shadows. Derwin refuses to traffic in the shallow, Christianized platitudes that plague so much of our modern discourse. Instead, with the tenderness of a seasoned pastor and the truth telling of a prophet, he invites us into the heavy, holy work of reckoning. Derwin calls us to be brutally honest about our pasts, to wade through the unavoidable turbulence of our pain, and to bravely accept our reality so that true, holistic renewal can begin. The crowning achievement of this book is its relentless drive toward liberation: learning to live an embodied life from the deep well of God's love rather than exhaustingly striving for it. If you are tired of the performance and ready to embrace the radical freedom of becoming a wounded healer, this book is a lifeline. *It's Time to Heal* is an essential guide for the journey toward wholeness.

LÉONCE B. CRUMP JR., founder and lead pastor of United Church

In *It's Time to Heal*, Pastor Derwin presents a powerful approach toward healing. The path he lays out comes from a place of deep faith, conviction, and humility. With clear, actionable steps that are illustrated by relatable, very human stories, the book shows readers the work they can do to find healing in their own lives. This book will certainly change lives.

JENNY MARRS, author of *Trust God, Love People* and cohost of HGTV's *Fixer to Fabulous*

Derwin has written an incredibly beautiful book! *It's Time to Heal* offers something both deeply pastoral and profoundly practical. With honesty and compassion, Derwin guides readers through the courageous work of healing, of naming what has happened, facing the pain, and choosing to live from love rather than fear. This book doesn't rush you. Derwin walks with you in a way that allows you to feel seen and supported in its pages. Poetic yet practical, rich in Scripture and grounded in wisdom, each chapter invites real transformation through reflection, prayer, and tangible next steps. If you are ready to heal not just in theory but in the deep reality of your everyday life, then this book will meet you there.

JO HARGREAVES, psychotherapist and host of *The Faith Filled Therapy Podcast*

In a world full of performance and pretending, Dr. Derwin Gray calls us back to truth. *It's Time to Heal* is a bold invitation to step out of denial and into real transformation. This book doesn't just expose the pain we hide—it points us to the Savior who can heal it. Don't simply turn these pages—let Jesus turn your story.

TIM TIMBERLAKE, lead pastor of Celebration Church and bestselling author of *The Bumpy Road to Better*

It's Time to Heal

FOUR GOD-GIVEN STEPS TO RESTORE WHAT LIFE HAS SHATTERED

DERWIN L. GRAY

NavPress
Published in alliance with Tyndale House Publishers

NavPress
Bold. Loving. Sensible.

NavPress.com

It's Time to Heal: Four God-Given Steps to Restore What Life Has Shattered

A NavPress resource published in alliance with Tyndale House Publishers

The Team:
David Zimmerman, Publisher; Caitlyn Carlson, Acquisitions Editor; Elizabeth Schroll, Copyeditor; Lacie Phillips, Production Assistant; Jennifer L. Phelps, Cover Designer; Brandi Davis, Interior Designer; Sarah Ocenasek, Proofreading Coordinator

Published in association with The Bindery Agency, thebinderyagency.com

For more resources from this author, see derwinlgray.com.

For information about special discounts for bulk purchases, please contact Tyndale House Publishers at csresponse@tyndale.com, or call 1-855-277-9400.

ISBN 979-8-89802-044-6

Printed in the United States of America

32 31 30 29 28 27 26
7 6 5 4 3 2 1

To my late father, Ruben Charles Wright.
It was impossible for me to know the depth of your wounds. But with older eyes shaped by the grace of God, I know you did the best you could.
Love you.

Contents

CHAPTER 0

Would You Like to Get Well?

Healing is holy, hard, and beautiful.
It's a collision of pain and glory.

Long ago, in a distant land, there lived a kind and wise man with a peculiar love for broken pots. While others walked past the garbage heaps without a second glance, he wandered among them, searching for treasures. With patience and tenderness, he sifted through what looked like trash to the untrained eye, piles of deformed metal and rotten food—until he caught a glimpse of the clay shards beneath. Then, with hands calloused by compassion, he carefully gathered the broken pieces and joyfully went to work. He bound the fragments together using a mixture of melted gold, turquoise, and emerald flecks. Slowly, painstakingly, he transformed what was once broken into an object of breathtaking beauty.

Some would watch him work and shake their heads. "That one's too far gone," they'd say. "Why not just throw it away?" But he would smile and reply, "A pot may be broken, but it's never beyond repair. All it needs is love and a little attention. Broken things can be beautiful."

Where most folks saw worthless rubble, he saw *potential.* Where others saw shattered pots, he saw *stories waiting to be redeemed.*

One day, a stranger came to him with their favorite pot and said, "Sir, this one's never been broken."

The compassionate man took the pot in his nail-pierced hands and turned it slowly, tracing the shimmering lines of gold, turquoise, and emerald that danced across its surface.

"Oh, but it has been broken," he said. "Years ago, when I found this one, it was shattered, buried deep beneath heaps of garbage. Maybe someone threw it on the floor in a fit of rage. Or perhaps this pot was neglected, dropped and forgotten, left unseen in fractured pieces. But it does not matter how broken a pot may seem, or what caused it to break. What you see now is the result of my love. I'm in the business of resurrecting what was once broken."

Cracked Pots

We are all cracked pots.

Broken by the fall.

Fractured by our own sin.

Crushed by the sin others committed against us.

Full of cracks that whisper regret and echo pain and shout shame.

But in the hands of the wise, kind Potter—the Father, the Son, and the Holy Spirit—our brokenness isn't wasted. It's *redeemed.* God himself, in his eternal Son, purchased our life with his own. The One who has always loved us doesn't run from our scars; he runs to us and shows us the scars on his hands, his feet, and his back. It's his scars that heal ours. It's his pain that heals ours. It's his strength that becomes ours.

Day after day, month after month, year after year, he keeps pursuing us, keeps mending what's broken. He's a Carpenter, a Potter, a Creator who never tires of shaping, carving, and repairing his children. His chasing of us stretches from eternity to eternity. Healing is a journey of God walking before us, beside us, and through us. As we journey with him and trust his faithful care, we begin to love the One who heals us more than the actual healing itself. The scars we once looked at with shame become testimonies of his mercy.

The longer the Carpenter holds us in his hands, even our cracks and fractures, the wounds and scars we carry, become proof that what the enemy thought would break us God has used to remake us. Your wounds are no longer marks of defeat; they are medals of honor. Your scars shout, "God brought me through!"

In the hands of the Potter, your scars and your trauma no longer define you. They tell a new story about the God who has given you a new name: *HEALED*.

H: Held in the Potter's hands.
E: Embraced even with your wounds.
A: Anointed with a new identity.
L: Loved into wholeness.
E: Empowered to rise again.
D: Defined by God, not your past.

Our hurt no longer has the greatest influence in our lives. Jesus does.

Our trauma is no longer the loudest voice in our heads. The Spirit of God is.

Our disappointments no longer dictate our lives. The Father's love does.

He Has Scars Too

I know someone else with scars. He has jagged holes in his wrists and feet where Roman nails once pinned him to a cross. His side bears a deep gash where a soldier's spear tore flesh to prove he had died. His back looks like a map of suffering, lacerated like crisscrossed train tracks.

Some might look at his scars and see failure and a tragic, brutal defeat. But those who've been reborn see them differently.

We see glory.
We see *grace*.
We see triumph.
We see healing.

> He was pierced because of our rebellion,
> crushed because of our iniquities;
> punishment for our peace was on him,
> and we are healed by his wounds.
>
> **ISAIAH 53:5**

For all eternity, Jesus' scars will remain, tattooed into his glorified, resurrected body. Not hidden. Not erased. Not forgotten. But *on display* as a living memorial, a sacred reminder to the redeemed of the price he paid to heal us. Every time we look at him, we will see love that bled for us. We will see the Lamb who was slain and who still bears the wounds of our healing.

Saving the Word *Saved*

What does it mean to be saved?

In the New Testament, the Greek word *sōzō* (σῴζω) means far more than going to heaven when we die. The saving, sanctifying love of the Father, the Son, and the Holy Spirit is continuously rescuing, healing, and purifying us to reflect Jesus. The grace of God never sleeps, never takes a day off, and is unrelenting in redeeming us so we can experience life to the full.

Sanctification is the patient work of God drawing us back to who we truly are: his beloved ones. Sanctification isn't driven by fear or pressure to perform for humans or God. It grows in the quiet places where we let ourselves be seen by God as we truly are. When we bring our wounds, our fears, and the lies we've believed into the light of Jesus, the sacredness of healing begins.

The Holy Spirit begins to soften what has grown hard and heal what has been broken. Little by little, he forms Christ in us. Day by day, he frees us from the lies we created to survive and awakens our true selves, whom God has always known and loved.

Sanctification is a lifelong journey of becoming whole, becoming authentic, becoming rooted in the love that will not let us go. In it God shapes us in such a way that our lives, our desires, and our hearts come to reflect Jesus, the One who calls us his own.

I have found that many people think of our ongoing

sanctification as an academic endeavor of acquiring more biblical knowledge. As a New Testament scholar, I love academic study, but if I do not allow the gospel I study to penetrate and integrate into my emotional wounds, I will remain stuck in my hurt. True sanctification doesn't gloss over pain or pretend that trauma didn't happen. It invites us to trust the Spirit of God to lead us into the deep, soul-level healing that equips us to look our scars in the eye and say, "I'm still here." "I'm moving forward." "I'm reclaiming the life God has meant for me to live." It brings the kind of healing that doesn't erase your story but honors every wound as evidence that you are more than a survivor because you are more than a conqueror in Christ.[1]

When Jesus saves us, he delivers us from the penalty of sin (past),[2] breaks the power of sin (present),[3] and one day, in the new heaven and new earth, he will free us from the very presence of sin (future).[4] Salvation is the beautiful, gracious act of God whereby he loves us so deeply that he forms the very life of Christ within us,[5] shaping us to become who we were always meant to be.

Salvation means that our God doesn't waste our pain. He is *Jehovah Rapha*, the God who heals. The apostle Paul says it this way: "Put on your new nature, created to be like God—truly righteous and holy."[6]

Like a gardener planting seeds, God plants the life of Christ in you. The Holy Spirit nurtures, teaches, and empowers you to live by faith as someone already made whole. Healing doesn't delete your scars. In the mystery of grace, God takes what was meant for evil against you and uses it for good in your life, making you "mature in Christ."[7]

This deep work of the Spirit isn't a quick fix. People are not like yesterday's leftovers that just need a quick spin in the microwave. Healing is the slow work of God in the hearts of the willing. It's a sacred, lifelong journey of walking with Jesus, the Wounded Healer. At times the path will twist, turn, and jolt like a roller coaster with a loose seat belt, leaving you breathless and gripping for stability. Some days it'll be as gentle as an autumn breeze, wrapping around you like a whispered promise of renewal. Healing is holy, hard, and beautiful. It's a collision of pain and glory.

One day, in the new heaven and new earth, you won't need healing anymore. What God declared over you when you first began to journey with him will finally become a reality, and you'll be fully whole.

No more tears.
No more suffering.
No more trauma.
No more brokenness.
Only beauty.
Only joy.
Only flourishing.

Do You Want to Get Well?

For thirty-eight years, a man laying by the pool of Bethesda had been ill. Thirty-eight years of waiting. Thirty-eight years of disappointment. So much time spent hoping someone would carry him to the water. Then Jesus showed up. "When Jesus saw him and knew he had been ill for a long time, he asked him, 'Would you like to get well?'"[8]

That is the question Jesus is asking you right now.

I'm inviting you to step into the healing waters God has already prepared for you. Jesus died and rose to give you abundant life. The days of settling for mere survival are over. The powers of darkness, the pain caused by others' sin, and your own foolish choices have stolen enough from you. It's time to get up and take back what hell has taken from you.

As a wounded healer and pastor, I count it a sacred honor to walk with you in the healing grace God offers. You're not walking this path alone. Along the way, you'll also hear from trusted friends in the mental health field in the "Counselors' Corner." The spiritual and sanctifying journey through our pain is vital. So is the way God reveals himself and shapes us through modern research and science. These wise guides will share practical insight and encouragement to help you take steps toward healing and wholeness.

Together in these pages, we're going to walk through four transformative truths about what God invites us into on the path to HEALing:

- **H**: *Honesty about what happened to you.* You cannot heal from what you will not name.
- **E**: *Expecting pain on the journey.* Healing is hard. But so is staying unhealed.
- **A**: *Accepting what happened (but not letting it define you).* Acceptance is not approval. It's refusing to let your past hold the pen that writes your future.
- **L**: *Living* from *love, not* for *love.* You are already loved. Live like it.

Today is a new day. It's time to heal and turn your scars into testimonies.

Prayer

Father,
You are the God who sees, who knows, who heals.
I surrender my past, my pain, and my plans.
And I take your hand, ready to walk,
step-by-step, into healing.

Jesus,
I hear you asking me, "Would you like to get well?"
And with trembling faith, I say: *Yes*.
I don't want to just manage my pain; I want to be healed.
I don't want to keep pretending. I want to live.

Holy Spirit,
Come into the places I've buried,
the wounds I've ignored,
the stories I've tried to forget.
Heal what's broken.
Redeem what was stolen.
Make me whole again.

In Jesus' healing name,
amen.

Reflection Questions

1. Which parts of your story still carry hurt when you touch them?

2. Where do you notice yourself reacting out of fear, distrust, or anger (even when you don't want to)? These tender places are not signs of failure. They're invitations. They reveal the areas of your life where Jesus is gently saying, "Let me heal this with you."

MY HEALING COMMITMENT

It's time to say yes to the healing journey.

> *I believe that Jesus can heal what has been broken in me. I believe that my scars can become testimonies. I will not waste another day waiting by the pool. I commit to reading this book with an open heart and to taking every step God calls me to take. By his grace, I will move toward healing.*
>
> *I am ready to heal.*
>
> *Signed:* ______________________________
>
> *Date:* ______________________________

PART 1

H:

Honesty About What Happened to You

You cannot heal from what you will not name.

CHAPTER 1

Hide No More

Healing begins when you name what happened.

In 1995, I was a team captain for the Indianapolis Colts. We were playing a critical game against the New Orleans Saints in New Orleans, and I played well, except for two personal penalties. One was questionable. The other one was on me. Both penalties were costly, and we lost the game. I was devastated—and I didn't have the emotional tools to process the loss.

Deep down, I wasn't just afraid of losing the game. I was terrified of losing my identity. If I lost my job as a football player, who would I be? I'd go back to being just the poor, stuttering boy from the west side of San Antonio if I wasn't an NFL player. I'd be a nobody from nowhere.

When we landed back in Indianapolis, I went to a restaurant bar with some teammates instead of going home. I got hammered trying to drown the fear I didn't want to face.

Meanwhile, my wife was at home pregnant and sick. She had a condition called hyperemesis gravidarum, which caused her to vomit constantly. She had been throwing up every day, all day, for months.

We didn't have cell phones back then, so she had no clue where I was and no way to reach me. Selfishness emboldened my shame. I didn't want to reach her. I wanted to gorge in self-pity.

A teammate carried me into my house that night. I stumbled down the hallway and into our bedroom, reeking of alcohol and regret. My wife looked at me and asked, "Where have you been?" I opened my mouth to speak, but vomit poured out instead. I dropped to my knees, sobbing, "I let you down. I let the team down. I let myself down."

But the truth was deeper. I had made football my god. I thought being a professional football player would heal the hurt parts of me. But when you worship a false god, it's never satisfied. It never delivers on its promises. It keeps demanding more. And when you fail it, it crushes you without mercy.

I passed out. My wife was too sick to clean up the mess. Her sister, who was taking care of her, cleaned up for me. The next morning I stood in the bathroom, staring at myself in the mirror. And that's when I said aloud, "Derwin, something is wrong with you."

When you don't know how to deal with pain, denial becomes your escape. But when I finally faced the truth, that was the beginning of leaving the River of Denial. The beginning of being honest with Jesus. He knew I was messed up. It was time for me to acknowledge that I was messed up.

Healing begins when we are honest with God about where we are.

Denial Won't Deliver You

The River of Denial always carries you somewhere painful. You can't heal when you won't deal with what happened to you. God only heals the true version of us. We may fool other people with our perfectly curated Instagram pages, but God knows the real us.

He knows the dark places we hide.

He knows our self-harm.

He knows the tears we shed. And he has bottled each one.[1]

Denial will never deliver you from your brokenness. Denial only delays your deliverance. Denial is a cruel abuser. It threatens, *If people really knew you or what happened to you, they would never love you.* Denial lies. And lies keep us in bondage. Only the truth can set us free. I know from experience that pretending protects our pain instead of helping us process it. Pain that goes unprocessed grows like a cancerous tumor. The surgery to remove the tumor will hurt, but the healing is worth it.

We can be completely honest with our Father in heaven. He knew us before time began. Before the sun smiled and the ocean waves roared, he knew everything about us. On the cross, Jesus suffered to take the burden of our sins and the burden of the effects of how people have sinned against us. He rose again to give us a new life that is defined no longer by our scars but by his scars. But you must come to him asking to be made well. Grace can only be poured into broken, needy hearts.

One of the reasons Alcoholics Anonymous is effective is because of step 1: "We admitted we were powerless over alcohol—that our lives had become unmanageable."[2] Healing starts with an admission that we need help. That's why Jesus' Step #1 for how to live in the Kingdom of God is "Blessed are the poor in spirit, for the kingdom of heaven is theirs."[3] Blessed are those who realize they can't heal themselves.

Don't walk past the Doctor's office. He's waiting for you to come in.

The Eye in the Sky

In the NFL, the day after a game is film review day. It is a brutally honest experience. Every team will film the game from multiple angles. NFL alumni call the film crew "the eye in the sky." The eye in the sky misses nothing. You can tell your teammates you played great. You can convince your family you played great. But the film often tells another story—the true story. Every mistake. Every success. It's all right there for you and all your teammates to see.

Before we gathered as a team, the coaches would watch the film and assign every player a grade for how they'd played in the game. Then, on Monday, we'd sit together in a dark room and watch every play from multiple angles. There was nowhere to hide. You'd feel exposed. But if you were humble, it could also be a moment of growth. You can't get better if you're not honest.

Facing the truth about ourselves doesn't have to be a place of shame. It can be a place of transformation. Jesus is the ultimate Eye in the Sky. He sees it all—not just the wrong we've done to others but also the wrong done to us. And when he grades our game films, he covers our sins with his blood. Through his resurrection, he gives us a new identity with an A+ grade.

Stop hiding from the film review with Jesus. He already knows. You can be honest with him. Let him be honest with you. His grace is big enough to heal you.

A Man Who Faced His Wounds

Can you imagine your own brothers hating you so intensely that they beat you, threw you into a pit, and then sold you into slavery? That they could be so jealous and angry that they'd lie to your father, telling him you were dead? That as proof they'd hand him the bloodstained coat he had lovingly handcrafted just for you?

Can you imagine being ripped from your home and sold into a foreign land, forced to serve under the rule of strangers? You give your best. You serve with integrity. And your faithfulness earns you leadership in your master's household, only to have it all stripped away again when his wife falsely accuses you of trying to violate her. You're unjustly thrown into prison. And there, in the darkness, you're betrayed again, this time by someone who promised to help you.

Years pass and *Jehovah Rapha*, the God who heals, redeems your suffering. The very gift he placed in you is the key that opens the prison doors to the gates of the palace. Now you are not just free, you are second-in-command of one of the most powerful empires on earth.

As you rise, your past still lingers like irritating background music. A famine hits the land. And while you're ascending, your brothers, who unleashed unspeakable pain in your life, are descending into desperation. Word spreads of a wise man in Egypt with food, a man who can save them. They come, hungry and hopeless. They stand before you, but they don't recognize you. You've changed. You're not a skinny boy anymore.

The hot sun has darkened your skin.

The hard labor of slavery has made you muscular and strong.

Your time of suffering has made you wiser, humbler, and more compassionate.

You were thrown in a pit.

Betrayed by family.

Falsely imprisoned.

Rejected and forgotten.

But it didn't break you. Loving and sovereign, God remade you into a better version of you. He didn't cause the pain, but he did reshape the pain they inflicted on you to work out for your good so you could save many lives, including the lives of those who tried to harm you.[4]

Instead of retribution, you give mercy.

You give grace because your pain was not wasted. God transformed it into purpose.

You show love because your suffering has shaped your soul so you're able to feel the suffering of others. You remember: God was always sovereign. What they meant for evil, God meant for good—to bring about the saving of many lives.[5]

Joseph's story hits something deep inside us. We're drawn to him because he rose above a dysfunctional family, betrayal, and years of unjust suffering. He went from the pit to the palace. But we miss the heart of the story if we overlook this: He didn't ignore his trauma. And because he chose to face what had happened to him, Joseph took three powerful steps toward healing. By faith, you and I can follow the same path.

Step #1: You Can't Heal What You Won't Reveal

Joseph didn't hide his wounds. He didn't bury the betrayal or sugarcoat the pain. He looked his past in the face and spoke the truth: "You sold me into slavery." His honesty opened the door to forgiveness. Healing never happens in the dark. When we name the pain, we take away its power and give God permission to start the healing.

Step #2: Forgiveness Takes Courage

Joseph's strength wasn't in his position of power. It was in his willingness to be vulnerable. Staying bitter does not require courage. But it takes courage to open your heart to trust, to forgive, to love. Joseph chose to speak truth with grace, and the floodgates of healing burst open. His courage didn't just heal him; it invited his brothers into honesty too. In this messy space of honesty and pain, reconciliation happened.

Step #3: God Doesn't Waste Your Pain; He Transforms It

The very brothers who once threw Joseph into a pit later bowed before him in Egypt. And Joseph, seasoned by God's wisdom and his trust in God's bigger picture, said to them, "God sent me ahead of you to preserve life."[6] It's like Joseph was saying to his brothers, "You put me through hell, and

God still won!" Joseph's pain became the provision that saved people. And from those people came the Savior of the world: Jesus.

The story of Joseph is really a story about God being faithful, loving, and great enough to take trauma and transform it into triumph. The powers of darkness don't want you to heal, because your healing will lead to the healing of others. Be courageous. God is with you. God is rewriting your story.

Prayer

Father,
I'm done hiding.
I'm done pretending.
I'm done thinking I can fix myself.

Jesus,
I need your healing touch.
Restore what's been broken, redeem what's been lost,
and make me whole.

Holy Spirit,
I trust you with my scars.
You're the Healer, who never wastes pain.
Give me courage to heal.

Amen.

Reflection Questions

1. What pain or struggle have you been hiding or denying?

   Be honest with yourself. What have you been afraid to face or speak out loud?

   Why have you felt the need to hide it? What have you been afraid would happen if it came into the light?

2. Write this truth in your journal: "Denial only delays your deliverance."

   What do those words mean to you personally?

   Can you think of a time when avoiding the truth only made your pain last longer?

   What would change if you stopped running and let God meet you right where you are?

CHAPTER 2

Head Home

You're not too far gone.

There once was a young man lavishly loved by his father. He lived in a home filled with everything he could desire: his father's protection, provision, dignity, and meaningful work. He even had an older brother to share it all with. But a restless voice began to tempt him: *Your father is holding you back.*

He started to believe his life was too small, too boring in his father's house. So one day, in a moment charged with selfishness, he turned to his father and said, "I want my inheritance. Now!"

In his culture, that request was unthinkable. An inheritance wasn't given until the father died. The young man's demand was as though he were saying, "I wish you were dead. I want what you worked hard to acquire." The whole village would've gasped in shock and disgust. Even his older brother stood in disbelief. But the father, heartbroken, did something no one expected. He said yes, divided his property, and gave the younger son his share. Doing this cost the father his social standing and honor in the community because his wealth was reduced. Even the older brother felt the blow because what the younger son took lessened what remained for him.

With a pocket full of cash and a head full of wild fantasies, the young man left home. He headed straight for the far country, where the Gentiles were known for sex-fueled parties and mind-altering drugs. At first, it was everything he'd imagined. He was finally free, or so he thought. But slowly, the lights began to dim. His money ran out fast. His new friends ran out on him faster. The illusion of freedom revealed what it really was: bondage.

This dude hit rock bottom.

Hungry and broken, he took the only job he could find: working on a pig farm. In his culture, if you worked with unclean pigs, you were an unclean religious failure. Day by day, he sloshed through mud and filth and shame. One day he woke up so hungry that he almost ate the pigs' food. Then he looked at himself in the reflection of the pigs' water trough—and he truly saw himself. How far he had come. How soiled in disgrace he was.

As he looked at this pitiful sight, he remembered his father's house. The warmth. The safety. The love. Even the hired workers at his father's estate had food to eat and a roof over their heads. He got up and began to make the long journey home. As he walked, he began rehearsing a speech of repentance: "Father, I've sinned against heaven and against you. I'm no longer worthy to be called your son. But maybe you could let me be a servant." He didn't expect a warm welcome. He just hoped for a little drop of mercy.

But what he didn't know was that his father had been watching and waiting for him to come home. The father scanned the horizon as the sun was setting, and he saw a familiar figure limping down the road. His son. In a moment of holy, reckless love, the father ran to his beloved child. An old, distinguished man would never run in this culture. Running meant lifting your robes, exposing your legs, risking shame. But love always runs faster than shame.

If the village elders had seen the boy first, they would have met him and stopped him at the village gate. They would have smashed clay pots at his feet, a symbolic act of rejection, and declared him exiled from the community. And so his father ran to him, as if each step were saying, "If you're going to smash anything on my precious son, you're going to have to smash it over me first."

He got to his son before the village elders. He threw his arms around his son's neck and kissed him. The boy tried to give his speech. He started: "Father, I've sinned against heaven and against you . . ." But his dad wasn't hearing any of it. He stopped his apology and called to the servants, "Quick!

"Bring the best robe.

"Bring my ring.

"Bring sandals for his feet.

"Bring the fattened calf and slaughter it. We're throwing a party tonight!"

That's what grace looks like when it runs to meet and kiss you. When the son came home, he was covered in shame and filth, rehearsing an apology. But the father didn't wait for the speech. He ran, embraced him, and poured out a love that looked like a kiss, a robe, a ring, shoes, and a fattened calf.[1]

- *The kiss.* With one kiss, the father silenced the shame. "I forgive you. I hold nothing against you."
- *The robe.* The father placed the best robe over his son's tattered clothes. This wasn't just warmth; it was covering. "You may feel dirty and unworthy, but I see you clothed in my honor."
- *The ring.* He slipped a ring on his son's finger as a sign of restored authority. "You're not a servant. You're still my son. You still carry my name."
- *The shoes.* Hired servants walked barefoot. Sons wore shoes. "You don't have to earn your way back. You belong here. You always have."
- *The calf.* He killed the fattened calf and threw a party. "We're not mourning your sin. We're celebrating your return."

This story isn't just about a wayward son. It's about the lavishly loving Father, who gives even when his son has done his worst. It's a story of how grace heals us.

Grace runs to us.

Grace hugs and kisses us.

Grace restores us.

Grace covers us.

Grace throws a feast in our honor.

God the Father, with a fistful of grace, is running toward you today.

You Can Come Home Too

I am the son who left home. And so are you. If we're honest, we'll admit that our own sin has wounded us deeper than anything others have done to us. We thought we were chasing freedom, but it led us to a pig farm of regret, shame, and guilt. Yet our Father hasn't turned his face away from us! Instead, he ran to meet us at the cross. With a kiss of mercy and the blood of his Son, he says, "You are forgiven. I remember your sins no more."[2] He wraps you in a robe of righteousness that was not earned but given as a gift. Now and for all eternity, when the Father looks at you, he sees you clothed in the perfection of Jesus.[3]

He slides shoes on your feet, proof you're not a servant but a beloved child.[4] And the ring is the Holy Spirit, his seal on your soul, his promise that you're a coheir with Christ, forever.[5]

So many of your wounds remain open because you've been stuck in a cycle of shame and guilt. Shame only ever leads you back to the pig farm. But your Father doesn't shame you for where you've been.[6] He celebrates because you've come home. "My child was dead—but now they are alive again!"

Grace meets us wherever we are. Sometimes we might be living in the Father's house yet still be far from his heart. The older brother never left home. He worked hard. He followed the rules. But when his broken, rebellious younger brother came back and the father threw a celebration, the older brother's true heart was revealed. Instead of rejoicing, he was angry. Bitter. Resentful. He refused to join the party. He stood outside, arms crossed, asking, *What about me?* He thought he had to earn what the Father had already promised. He didn't realize that everything the Father owned had always been his. Isn't that tragic? He spent his whole life in the house but never knew the joy of his father's love.

That's what happens when we live without grace. We strive for God's approval. We work ourselves weary trying to earn what's already ours in Christ. We exhaust ourselves trying to heal ourselves. And we miss the party.

The Father is pleading with you: "Everything I have is already yours. Stop working for what grace already gave you. Come inside. Celebrate with me."

Your healing isn't something you have to earn. It's a gift you receive by faith, and little by little, from glory to glory, healing happens.

Come back.

And stay home.

Everything you need is already in the Father's house.

Grace lives there. And so can you.

Prayer

Father,
I've wandered in shame
and lived far from your love.
But today I've come home.
Thank you for running to me,
covering my failures with grace,
and reminding me I'm always your child.
I receive your robe, your ring, your shoes, and your joy.

Jesus,
Heal what shame broke.
Fill what sin emptied.
Restore what guilt stole.

Holy Spirit,
Remind me that I'm never too far gone, and lead me home.

Amen.

Reflection Questions

1. Have you been living like the younger son in a far country or like the older brother—in the Father's house but far from his heart?

2. If you were to write a letter to God thanking him for his grace, what would you write?

CHAPTER 3

Heal Your Heart

Guard your heart above all else,
for it is the source of life.
PROVERBS 4:23

Let me tell you a story about a quiet town in a place so beautiful it'd take your breath away. It was the kind of town that, once you spent time there, you wouldn't want to leave. You'd start looking at real estate listings. The people were kind and generous. Wisdom was passed down from generation to generation. The air was fresh, the sky a deep blue, the trees full and green. Everything just felt right.

But over time, something changed. The people began to get sick. First it was the children, then the elderly. Soon young adults started to fall ill too. As the years passed, everyone born in that town carried some form of sickness. No one knew why until one day someone had an idea. "What if it's the river?" The town's environmental agency tested it and found toxic chemicals. The water they drank, bathed in, and built their lives around was toxic. Slowly, silently, it had been poisoning everything and everyone, even deforming their DNA.

Upstream, hidden deep in the woods, was an industrial plant. For decades, the waste from the plant had flowed into the river, infecting the lifeblood of the town. People died. Despair took root. Violence broke out. The land itself seemed to wear a funeral veil.

The Better Adam

This is the story of how sin entered creation. Because of Adam's sin in the ancient garden, we are all born sick.

> Therefore, just as sin entered the world through one man, and death through sin, in this way death spread to all people, because all sinned.
>
> **ROMANS 5:12**

We weren't just born sick with sin. We spread that sickness too. Our wounds wound others. Our brokenness breaks others.

What are we to do? We need a new source of water to drink that heals us.

Jesus is that water source. He says, "If you knew the gift of God, and who is saying to you, 'Give me a drink,' you would ask him, and he would give you living water."[1] Think of it this way:

Adam poisoned us. Jesus gave us the antidote.

Adam wounded us. Jesus was wounded to heal us.

Adam hid behind a tree. Jesus hung on a tree.

Adam broke us. Jesus made us whole.

Adam gave us death. Jesus gave us life.

Jesus is better than Adam. He is the eternal water source, who hydrates us with his life.

> If by the one man's trespass, death reigned through that one man, how much more will those who receive the overflow of grace and the gift of righteousness reign in life through the one man, Jesus Christ.
>
> **ROMANS 5:17**

The moment we drink in the living water, the old is gone, and we become a new creation in Christ.[2] We are healed at the deepest level of our being. Not just improved. Not just patched up. Made new.

If That's True

Honestly, though, early in my faith, I wrestled with some questions that maybe you're asking too:

- *If I'm a new creation, why am I still a mess?*
- *If I'm a new creation, why do I still feel so insecure?*
- *If I'm a new creation, why can't I forgive myself?*
- *If I'm a new creation, why am I so angry all the time?*
- *If I'm a new creation, why can't I break this cruel cycle of addiction?*
- *If I'm a new creation, why do I keep doing the very things I said I'd never do again?*

Even the apostle Paul, who wrote much of the New Testament, cried out in frustration and honesty:

> I don't understand what I do. For what I want to do, I don't do. But what I hate—I do.
>
> **ROMANS 7:15, AUTHOR'S PARAPHRASE**

On August 2, 1997, when I met Jesus and he forgave me, something miraculous happened. He instantly made me new at the core of who I was. The Bible says I was given a *new heart.* In Hebrew, the word *heart* (*lēb*; לֵב) doesn't just mean "emotions." It's the control center of the entire person: our intellect, emotions, will, and desires. God promised this long ago:

> I will give you a new heart and put a new spirit within you; I will remove your heart of stone and give you a heart of flesh. I will place my Spirit within you and cause you to follow my statutes and carefully observe my ordinances.
>
> **EZEKIEL 36:26-27**

But while my *heart* was made new in an instant, my *mind* needed transforming. My ingrained habits needed to be rehabbed. I've come to realize that becoming a new creation happens in an instant but learning to live as a new creation takes a lifetime. This Holy Spirit–initiated and –empowered process is called sanctification (the process of growing in holiness). It's the daily trusting and surrendering the totality of our lives to the Holy Spirit's influence as he shapes us to reflect Jesus.

Guard Your Heart, Rewire Your Mind

Solomon, the wisest man to walk the earth before Jesus, gave us this advice: "Guard your heart above all else, for it is the source of life."[3] Why must you guard your heart? Because it's the battlefield for your life. Your heart is where the wounds from your past try to dictate and destroy your future. It's where lies try to override God's truth. It's where fear tries to crush your faith. But it's also where you are "strengthened with power in your inner being through his Spirit . . . that Christ may dwell in your hearts through faith."[4]

Your heart is where healing begins and heaven touches earth. God's gift to us is far too precious to neglect. You must guard your heart by renewing your mind with the riches of God's grace.

Modern neuroscience is catching up with what the Bible has proclaimed for centuries: Your mind *can* be transformed. Neuroscientist Dr. Daniel Amen says, "Your brain is continually reorganizing itself by forming new neural connections throughout your life, which gives you the power to make your brain better."[5] The Cleveland Clinic describes this reorganization, known as neuroplasticity, as "an internal rewiring process that allows your mind to grow and meet new and increased demands."[6]

But long before science gave it a name, Scripture gave us a promise: "Do not be conformed to this age, but be transformed by the renewing of your mind."[7]

Jesus is inviting you to guard your heart by renewing your mind with the truth of the gospel. For years, intrusive and destructive lies have tormented you. Dark thoughts have carved highways into your brain, leading straight into cul-de-sacs of shame, fear, and despair. But Jesus has built a new road for your thoughts to travel. It's time to exit the road of despair and get on the freeway of grace, where the light shines, the truth heals, and the path leads you home to the heart of God.

Christ Behavioral Therapy

Several years ago, I was introduced to cognitive behavioral therapy (CBT).[8] What I love about it is how simple and practical it is. CBT helps us see that the thoughts we hold eventually shape the emotions we feel and those emotions shape how we show up in the world. When our thinking gets twisted by pain, shame, or old wounds, our lives start to follow twisted patterns.

But here's the hope: Those patterns of thinking can be healed. With the right help, we can learn to recognize the thoughts that are hurting us and invite God's truth into those spaces. We can unlearn the habits that were once for surviving but now keep us from thriving. CBT gives people tools to slow down, name what's really going on inside, and step into healthier ways of living. It helps us understand ourselves and others with more clarity and compassion. And as we practice these skills under the influence of the Holy Spirit, confidence grows. Healing grows. Freedom grows.

In God's hands, CBT becomes one more way he renews our minds and restores our lives, one thought at a time.

There's a spiritual reality in all this. I call it Christ behavioral therapy. It's rooted in this passage from Colossians:

> If you have been raised with Christ, seek the things above, where Christ is, seated at the right hand of God. Set your minds on things above, not on earthly things. For you died, and your life is hidden with Christ in God.
>
> **COLOSSIANS 3:1-3**

In high school, our football coaches drilled the playbook into us so deeply that when adversity occurred, we focused on knowing and executing the plays, not the adversity. We had trained our minds to respond to the playbook, not the hardship. That's what we do with our hearts and minds as God begins to heal us.

The gospel version of CBT means that you do these things:

- *Reframe your identity.* You are God's beloved child. He eternally delights in loving you.
- *Refocus your thoughts.* Fix your mind on who Jesus is and his victory, not the adversity.
- *Rehearse your position.* You're raised from death and hidden in, clothed in, and empowered by Christ.

Reframe Your Identity

As a young girl, Ava[9] was bullied for how she looked. Cruel words cut deeper than anyone knew, tattooing shame into her soul. The pain became so overwhelming she switched schools, hoping for relief. But the punishing voices followed her and carved cruel words deep into her mind. The lies echoed louder and louder, wounding her from the inside out. Ava's self-worth was crushed.

And then at age fourteen she was sexually assaulted. Trauma upon trauma. Her self-worth plummeted even more. Ava replayed the lies in her mind like a song on repeat: *I'm hideous. I'm disgusting. I'm worthless. I'd be better off dead.*

I remember hearing as a boy, "Sticks and stones may break my bones, but words will never hurt me." But that's not true. Physical wounds often heal, but words can take up residence in our thoughts and stories and how we see the world. Words can make us soul sick when we allow them to define our identity. For Ava, little by little, the seeds of the lies turned into weeds that took over her life.

From ages fourteen to twenty-four, Ava couldn't look in the mirror without breaking down in tears. No medication, no amount of money, no designer clothes or new hairstyles could cover the deep ache inside. She wasn't chasing beauty; she was desperate for worth. But nothing worked. She was suffocating under the weight of the trauma.

The Greek origin of *trauma* means "wound."[10] It's more than just a painful moment. Trauma is not just something that happened to you. It is what happens inside you when suffering overwhelms your capacity to cope, leaving echoes in your emotions, your thinking, and even your body. At its heart, trauma does two devastating things: It makes you feel powerless, and it disconnects you from yourself, from others, and sometimes even from God.[11] Gabor Maté and

Daniel Maté write, "Whether we realize it or not, it is our woundedness, or how we cope with it, that dictates much of our behavior, shapes our social habits, and informs our ways of thinking about the world."[12]

For ten years, Ava lived in torment, leading to self-harm and multiple suicide attempts. Trauma wrapped itself around every lie the dark powers whispered in Ava's heart. She had no defense against it. She didn't know the truth of God's Word. She didn't yet know her identity and worth in Christ. She didn't realize the God of heaven was weeping with her, longing to heal her, fighting for her.[13]

Even though Ava was going to church and wore the outer clothing of religion, she was dying on the inside. Mental health struggles were a constant battle. She was exhausted from trying to fix herself in her own strength. The harder she tried, the more broken she became.

Ava's story isn't just hers. It's all of ours. Because the truth is that we're all walking wounded. When we make our wounds our identity, we spend a lot of time trying to manage the wounds alone. *This is who I am*, we think. *I've got this under control.* Some of us try to heal our shattered self-worth through casual hookups, hoping someone else's touch will silence the pain. Others numb the agony with drugs, alcohol, long hours at work, or hours lost in a gaming haze. Some of us try to win God's approval by doing more, serving more, performing more, while secretly knowing we're falling apart. We just want anything that will help us escape the chaos in our minds and feel some measure of control. Eventually, we all run out of strength. When we reach the end of our self-reliance, Jesus can begin.

We must hit rock bottom to discover Jesus, the Rock at the bottom. That's what happened to Ava. In February of 2024, she entered a Christ-centered residential home for women battling life-controlling struggles. Nine months later, she walked out transformed. Not because her pain vanished overnight but because Jesus met her in the deepest place of her pain and began to reframe her identity from the inside out.

Refocus Your Thoughts

One of the most life-changing graces Ava experienced in the residential home was a simple yet profound practice: creating truth statement cards. Each card carried a verse of Scripture that declared who she is in Christ.

Truths like these:

- I am loved.[14]
- I am chosen.[15]
- I am forgiven.[16]
- I am God's child.[17]
- I am his temple.[18]
- I am his righteousness.[19]
- I am redeemed.[20]
- I am a new creation.[21]
- I am God's masterpiece.[22]

At first, it felt awkward, just about impossible, to speak those healing words over herself. The lies had been loud for so long that it was hard to hear and believe God's promises. But surrounded by the love of the staff and the encouragement of her community, Ava began the holy practice of declaring God's truth over herself, even when she didn't believe it. She searched the Scriptures, and by faith took hold of this spiritual reality that Paul describes:

> We are human, but we don't wage war as humans do. We use God's mighty weapons, not worldly weapons, to knock down the strongholds of human reasoning and to destroy false arguments. We destroy every proud obstacle that keeps people from knowing God. We capture their rebellious thoughts and teach them to obey Christ.
>
> **2 CORINTHIANS 10:3-5, NLT**

Ava went to war for her mind and heart with a simple stack of index cards. On one side, she wrote the lies she had believed for years, lies like "I'm unlovable," "I'm too damaged," or "I'm disgusting." On the other side, she wrote the truth of who she is in Christ, anchored in Scripture: "I am God's beloved," "I am a new creation." With every card, she was rewriting her story, replacing shame with grace and lies with the healing power of God's Word. For the next eight months, she read and prayed through just three of these cards every single day out loud with bold faith. She'd say: "I reject the lie that I am disgusting. I receive the truth that I am God's masterpiece in Christ. God, thank you that your Word is true. Help me believe it, even when I don't feel it."

As Ava faithfully declared these truths, something remarkable began to happen. The Holy Spirit, working through the power of God's Word, began to rewire her mind. Through the gift of neuroplasticity, new neural pathways were formed, pathways built not on shame but on grace, not on lies but on love.

Rehearse Your Position

Ava describes her transformation as being like walking a new trail on a mountain path. For years, she had walked the same dark road, carved deep by self-hatred and lies. But now, by God's grace, she stopped going down that old road and started walking a new one.

At first, it was hard and painful. But over time, as days turned into weeks and weeks into months, the new trails became clearer and stronger. The old trail started to be covered over with weeds, slowly fading from view.

Ava now serves on the staff of a church, helping others find healing. She is a wounded healer. The pain that was meant to shatter her became the very place God began to shape her. What was meant to destroy her, God used to deliver her. From the ashes of her suffering, he raised up a woman of fierce compassion. She recently married a young man who grew up in the ministry of the church she now serves.

The Holy Spirit takes the truth of God, revealed through Jesus, and rewires our minds with grace. New pathways are formed. Old lies lose their power. Our minds become places of peace instead of chaos, strongholds of truth instead of confusion, gardens of mercy instead of shame.

But this doesn't happen by accident. In the Holy Spirit's power, renewing your mind takes daily intentionality. We must choose daily to take every thought captive to make it obey Christ.[23] Healing begins when our thoughts come under the rule of grace. As my daughter says, "Healing is not linear. Be patient with yourself."

The pain of the past doesn't fit your new heart. Guard your heart because Jesus bled, died, and rose to make it whole. Guard your heart because the Holy Spirit dwells in you. Guard your heart because from it flows the very essence of your life.[24]

Healing is more than the absence of pain. It's the presence of something new: God's heart beating within you. It's time for you to live from a new script. Jesus said, "You will know the truth, and the truth will set you free."[25]

Prayer

Father,
You are the truth that shatters every lie.
You are the Healer of wounded hearts
and the Restorer of shattered worth.
Today I bring you the parts of me that feel
broken, ashamed, and forgotten.
Like Ava, I've tried to fix myself. I've worn masks.
I've believed the voices that said I was unlovable,
unworthy, too far gone.
But no more.

Jesus,
I reject the lies that have haunted my soul.
I reject the shame that says I'm not enough.
I reject the darkness that tells me I'll never be whole.
And I receive your truth:
That I am loved.
That I am chosen.
That I am forgiven.
That I am your Father's child.
That I am his masterpiece.

Holy Spirit,
Rewire my heart and mind.
Let new paths of grace, truth, and life be carved into me.
Help me speak what is true, even when I don't feel it.

Help me believe what you say about me more than
what my past or pain try to say.
Thank you that when I hit rock bottom, I find you,
the Rock at the bottom.
And in you, I rise.

Amen.

Reflection Questions

1. Are you drinking from the river of shame or the well of grace?

   Take these steps:

   a. Name the toxic thoughts you've believed about yourself. Lies like *I'm too broken*, *I'll never change*, or *I'm unworthy*.
   b. Replace them with gospel truth. Write down Scriptures that speak to your identity in Christ (like Romans 8:1 and 2 Corinthians 5:17) and meditate on them daily.
   c. Speak grace out loud. When shame whispers, respond aloud with who Jesus says you are. Let your own voice echo heaven's declaration.

2. Have you trained your mind to guard your new heart?

   Take the following steps. Begin your day with Christ behavioral therapy. Practice Colossians 3:1-3 each morning:

   a. Reframe your identity: *I am God's beloved.*

b. Refocus your thoughts: *Jesus is on the throne, and his power and victory are in me.*
c. Rehearse your position: *I'm hidden, raised, and empowered in Christ.*

COUNSELORS' CORNER

True North

JIM CRESS (MA, LPC, CSAT, CMAT)

In my counseling work with people, I often use metaphors. One of my favorites is that of a compass. When I hold my beautifully crafted compass in my hand, I show someone I am working with all its points. Most important on this direction-pointing device is what is called *magnetic north*. This is the place on the compass that points magnetically toward the geographic North Pole. This is crucially important for someone seeking direction on a journey. However, magnetic north is not the same as *true north*. What is the difference? True north is the precise geographical fixed point where the earth is rotating, centered on the "top of the world" at the North Pole. Magnetic north on a compass changes over time; magnetic fields are influenced by the earth's shifting molten core.

In the Christian life, I equate magnetic north with my own best thinking or the "wisdom" and counsel of others who may not be aligned with God and his Word. In contrast, I relate true north with the omnipotent, omniscient wisdom, direction, and counsel of God. I regularly point people to

1 Kings 22:5, where King Jehoshaphat instructs King Ahab to "first seek the counsel of the LORD" (NIV).

God the Father, the Lord Jesus Christ, and the Holy Spirit are a Christian's true north. Magnetic north might offer helpful guidance from time to time, but when any human counsel (including our own) does not line up with God's wisdom and counsel in his Word, always seek the counsel of the Lord.

CHAPTER 4

Hope at the Well

When lies take root, truth sets you free.

The sun was scorching hot as the woman walked alone to the town well to draw water. That may not sound strange to you, but two thousand years ago in the city of Sychar in Samaria, this was unusual. Most women went to the well early in the morning or in the evening, when temperatures were cooler. But this woman—let's call her Sammie—arrived at noon, when no one else would be there. Did she go then because she preferred to be alone? Or because she was trying to avoid the other women of the city?

But on this day, Sammie wasn't alone. A Jewish rabbi named Jesus was sitting there, waiting for her. What he did next shocked her.

First, Jesus spoke to Sammie and asked her for a drink of water. In the first-century Jewish culture of Jesus' day, it was unthinkable for a Jewish man, especially a rabbi, to speak publicly to a woman. And even more shocking, this woman was a Samaritan. Jews and Samaritans had a nine-hundred-year history of racial and religious hostility. When Jesus opened his mouth to speak to her, it wasn't just a conversation—it was something revolutionary. He was breaking through deep-seated barriers of sexism, prejudice, and shame.

Sammie said, "How is it that you, a Jew, ask for a drink from me, a Samaritan woman?"

And Jesus replied, "If you knew the gift of God, and who is saying to you, 'Give me a drink,' you would ask him, and he would give you living water." Jesus glanced at the well. "Everyone who drinks from this water will get thirsty again. But whoever drinks from the water that I will give him will never get thirsty again. In fact, the water I will give him will become a well of water springing up in him for eternal life."

Her curiosity grew: "Give me this water so that I won't get thirsty and come here to draw water."

And Jesus gently responded, "Go call your husband."

"I don't have a husband," she answered.

"You have correctly said, 'I don't have a husband,'" Jesus said. "For you've had five husbands, and the man you now have is not your husband."[1]

Often, we rush to judgment of Sammie.

She must have been an immoral woman.

She must have been a prostitute.

But maybe Sammie wasn't licentious.

Maybe she was wounded.

In a world where men could divorce women for almost any reason, maybe she was the victim of ill-treatment from men.

Maybe the man she lived with didn't marry her because she had no dowry, no status, no worth in his eyes.

Maybe she was just trying to survive.

But what matters most is this: Sammie didn't lie. She was honest about her wounds. And in return, Jesus didn't shame her; he revealed himself to her. She saw the Messiah face-to-face. How beautiful.

The first person in the New Testament to whom Jesus revealed his identity as the Messiah wasn't a powerful political figure, an elite religious leader, or a devout Jew. It was an unseen Samaritan woman who was living with a man who was not her husband.

In a culture that silenced and sidelined women like her, Jesus made her one of the first messengers of his gospel. That's not a coincidence. That's the heart of God.

Sammie left her water jar, the reason she had come to the well, and ran back to the people she was avoiding. Why? Because she had tasted living water. Her soul, once dry and brittle from rejection and shame, was now hydrated with hope and healing.

Sammie shared about the source of her newfound hope, and as a result, the townspeople declared, "We no longer believe because of what you said, since we have heard for ourselves and know that this really is the Savior of the world."[2]

Come to the Well

Sammie's story is our story. As you choose to be honest about what happened to you, Jesus wants to offer to you what he did to her: four healing graces that lead to hope:

1. *Jesus saw her.* In a world where men ignored women, especially women like her, Jesus saw Sammie. He saw her pain. He saw her worth. He saw her shattered story. And Jesus sees you. He sees you in your hiding. He sees the tears no one else sees. He knows the shame you carry, the burdens you've never spoken out loud. He doesn't turn away. He turns to you and calls you to come drink from his well of unending grace.

   On the cross, he stepped into your suffering and bore it with you. He sympathizes with and understands you more than anyone else does. He has a cup of living water just for you.

2. *Jesus restored her dignity.* The eternal Son of God, the Creator of the universe, asked her, a Samaritan woman with a messy past, for a drink of water. In doing so, Jesus lifted Sammie up. He gave her value in a culture that treated her like she was disposable. Jesus made Sammie feel like somebody because to him she *was* somebody. And so are you.

   When God redeems you, he doesn't just erase your sin; he restores your dignity. He heals the piercing pain caused by the people who hurt you. He heals the wounds of shame and covers you in his worth. You don't get your dignity from climbing a spiritual ladder up to God. You get it from the God who climbed down from heaven to offer you living water.

3. *Jesus spoke truth wrapped in grace.* Jesus didn't ignore Sammie's sin. He didn't pretend her pain or

brokenness didn't exist. But he didn't condemn her either. He spoke truth and compassion. He brought her from hurt to healing. How do we know? Because she left her water jar at the well and took off running to tell the people about the Messiah. That jar was more than clay. It was a symbol of her sins and her past hurts.

4. *Jesus gave her a new purpose.* Sammie came to the well hiding in shame, but she left running with joy. She became one of the first evangelists in the New Testament. A woman the town had written off became a witness the town couldn't ignore. She met the Healer, and she couldn't keep it to herself.

   Jesus wants to do the same with you. He wants to make you a wounded healer, a living testimony that his love restores our dignity and launches us into our purpose of leading others to the well where Jesus hangs out.

Your wounds, your shame, the things that have defined you and diminished you—those are the jar you're carrying. You've been looking for all sorts of water to soothe the pain. But Jesus offers living water. When you face your pain honestly, Jesus enters and offers hope.

What water jar do you need to leave at the well?

- The jar of shame?
- The jar of porn?
- The jar of bitterness?

- The jar of poor boundaries?
- The jar of unforgiveness?
- The jar of sexual immorality?
- The jar of low self-worth?

Whatever your jar is, leave it at the well.

Prayer

Father,
In Christ
you met Sammie with compassion.

Jesus,
You see the parts of me I try to hide,
the wounds I've buried, the jars I carry,
the thirst I can't seem to quench.
But you don't turn away.
You turn toward me.

Holy Spirit,
Today I come to the well to drink
water that restores.
Water that dignifies.
I lay my jar at your feet;
I want to be healed.

In Jesus' name,
amen.

Reflection Questions

1. Are you willing to leave your water jar at the well so you can run freely into your God-given future?

   Name the jar you've been carrying.

   Tell Jesus you're ready to leave it at the well.

   Then take one bold step today that reflects your freedom. Share what you are learning in a social media post.

2. Where in your life have you learned to hide, and what would it look like to let Jesus meet you there without fear?

COUNSELORS' CORNER

Come to the Well

JIM CRESS (MA, LPC, CSAT, CMAT)

I often find with those I am counseling a familiar pattern of searching for an external solution to their internal problem. I reference the story of the woman at the well in John 4. In this beautiful narrative, Jesus continues to pursue the deep longings and thirsts of this woman's heart and soul while she repeatedly stays in her head, responding to Jesus cognitively about history and religion and affirming Jesus for his brilliant prophetic gifting. It is not until Jesus patiently, wisely begins to ask her about her life story that this precious woman begins to get in touch with her inner world and realizes that Jesus sees deeply into her. Indeed, he knows her. Shame was no doubt a toxic companion to this woman. I use an acrostic for the word *shame*: *s*elf-*h*atred *a*t *m*y *e*xpense. When we are living in shame, we experience the hatred of ourselves, and this self-hatred costs us significantly. Our shame will also harm and hinder our relationships with others and with God. This negative neuroplasticity works against our own mental and spiritual health to keep us trapped in what C. S. Lewis referred to as "the prison of [the] self."[3] When shame or toxic thoughts attack our minds, we must make the resilient choice to return—again and again—to the powerful liberation from all sin and negative, shameful, toxic self-talk found in Romans 8:1: "Therefore, there is now no condemnation for those in Christ Jesus."

PART 2

E:
Expecting Pain on the Journey

Healing is hard. But so is staying unhealed.

CHAPTER 5

Expect Turbulence

The pain of healing is better than the pain of staying hurt.

I love my grandmother. She passed away in 2005, but I still catch myself wanting to pick up the phone to tell her all the incredible things God is doing in my life. Her memory lives in me. And honestly, some of what she passed down, I carry still—both the beautiful and the dysfunctional.

One of those things is her fear of flying. My grandmother was terrified of airplanes, and without meaning to, she passed that fear on to me. Now imagine if I'd let that fear win. I would've missed flying from San Antonio to Dallas to play in the 1988 Texas high school state football championship. I would've missed four trips to Hawaii to play college football; the flights all over the country in the NFL; and the adventures I went on to preach the gospel in India, Korea, Germany, Norway, Israel, Spain, and Greece.

But there was this one flight over the Midwest from Los Angeles to Charlotte that I'll never forget. A storm rolled in. Turbulence rocked the plane like a roller coaster. The storm made the plane bounce violently.

Suddenly the plane dropped. People shot out of their seats and hit the ceiling. Screams filled the cabin. Somehow a tiny Chihuahua just trotted calmly down the aisle. It was chaos.

But fear didn't paralyze me this time. Deep down, I knew we were going to land safely.

Emotional healing is a lot like flying through a storm. It's not smooth. Often, it's scary, filled with moments where you feel completely out of control. There will be times when you will want to get off the plane because healing hurts. But don't let the turbulence convince you to stay stuck on the ground, trapped in your hurt. You will eventually land. You will make it home.

> I am sure of this, that he who started a good work in you will carry it on to completion until the day of Christ Jesus.
>
> **PHILIPPIANS 1:6**

You can trust the One who leads you through the turbulence. He is with us in the storms, keeping us near, holding us tight until the storms calm down.

When Pain Feels like Defeat

In my third season with the Indianapolis Colts, I was named special teams captain. I had a solid season, helping our defense climb to a number-seven ranking in the entire NFL. We were one game away from the Super Bowl, but in the final moments of the 1995 AFC Championship Game, the Pittsburgh Steelers ended that dream. Still, my career was on the rise, and expectations were high for me and the Colts in the 1996 season. I was ready for a breakthrough. But the only thing that began to break was my body.

Over the next three seasons, I tore my medial collateral ligament (MCL) in my left leg three times. I suffered multiple concussions. I tore the ligaments in my left ankle and broke my left leg. My body was falling apart. The rehab was brutal. Sometimes it felt like the healing process hurt worse than the original injury. But those painful days in rehab taught me something I'll never forget: The pain of healing is better than the pain of staying injured.

The same is true when it comes to our hearts, souls, and minds. The gospel unearths lies we've grown to treat as pets instead of enemies. Going to therapy hurts. Counseling can stir up wounds you've buried. But staying unhealed is even more costly. You don't just pay that price alone; the people who love you pay for it too. I've heard it said that hurt people hurt people. After nearly thirty years of walking with people through their deepest pain and struggles, I've seen this truth proven repeatedly. But it doesn't have to stay that way.

Healing takes courage! But you don't have to find that courage alone. The never-ending, life-giving love of God will carry you to healing. His Spirit will strengthen you. And it's worth every tear, every step, every scar. The pain you face today can break chains tomorrow—not just for you but also for future generations.

Scar Tissue

When your muscles get torn or damaged, your body doesn't just leave the wound open—it gets to work knitting things back together with scar tissue. Scar tissue is made of collagen, a strong, fibrous protein that holds bones together, supports tendons and ligaments, and repairs skin and organs. It's how the body rebuilds what's been broken and says, "I'm healing." Scar tissue is proof that healing is happening.[1]

You've probably heard people say, "You just have to break up the scar tissue." But that's a myth. The goal isn't to break it up but to remodel it. During rehab for my torn MCL, the team trainers would take me to the field so I could learn to run again and make sharp cuts, just like I would in an actual football game. As I did, I would feel the tightness in my left MCL, and at first, I thought I'd retorn the ligament. But what I thought was a reinjury was a natural part of healing. To heal well, scar tissue needs guidance, like manual stretch therapy, joint mobility exercises, soft tissue massage, and myofascial release.[2] You must work *with* the scar tissue, not fight against it.

Emotionally, we all have scar tissue. Life wounds us through trauma, betrayal, sin, or loss. In the same way physical scar tissue does, our emotional scar tissue needs rehab—like spiritual disciplines; friends mentoring; and at times, therapy. Jesus meets us through wise, caring people.

The scars in your soul will become signs of healing, reminders that even though you were hurt, you didn't stay hurt. You're still here. Still standing. Still healing.

Pain That Heals

I met Shae[3] about three years ago, after she and her new husband started worshiping at Transformation Church. From the very beginning, they jumped right in, serving in ministries and making friends. Shae's personality is magnetic. She is funny and full of light, and when you meet her you can't help but think, *I've got to be friends with her!* But as I got to know Shae, I also came to know her pain.

As a little girl, Shae was abused by her stepfather for several years. By the time she was a teenager, the pain inside her had turned into rage, and that rage showed up in school hallways. She was constantly fighting. She didn't know how to handle the hurt inside her. Every punch was really a cry for help.

Shae numbed the pain with drugs and unhealthy relationships. She tried anything she thought could silence the voice that told her she was worthless, dirty, and unlovable. Eventually, Shae was shipped off to a school for troubled teens.

Nothing worked until she met Jesus.

Shae came to faith in Christ, but her journey to healing was just beginning. When I met her, she was running hard, working multiple jobs, pouring herself into nonstop busyness. The busier she was, the less time she had to think about her trauma. On the outside, it looked like ambition. But on the inside, it was desperation.

If I'm good enough, Shae thought, *maybe people won't leave me. Maybe I won't be abused. Maybe someone will finally value me. Maybe if I was a better person, my stepfather wouldn't have hurt me.*

But people pleasing is a toxic, addictive drug. It promises love but steals your soul.

Shae joined the staff at our church, and my wife and I took her under our wing and began to disciple her. We walked with her through the journey of replacing lies with gospel truth, of learning to receive grace instead of guilt, kindness instead of performance-based acceptance. She also began working with a trauma-informed therapist who attends our church.

Real healing isn't passive.

It's the deep, painful work of shaping our emotional scar tissue.

It's a fight.

A holy fight.

And Shae showed up for it with people who love her.

Over time, through discipleship, therapy, and the love of a gospel-shaped community, she began the process of healing. She began to reclaim her life so it was no longer defined by her trauma but by the redeeming love of Jesus.

She's said to me more than once, "I had no idea healing would hurt this much. And I had no idea I could be healed this much."

Shae is one of the kindest, most loving people I've ever met. She has a burning passion to help other hurting people find wholeness in Christ. She loves introducing people to the healing power of Jesus. And it's beautiful.

Shae's scars aren't signs of defeat.
They're living testimonies of God's grace.
And so are yours.

Jesus Meets You in PAIN

On my most painful days of rehabbing my knee, I kept reminding myself that the pain of healing is better than the pain of staying hurt. Because PAIN is the place where Jesus meets you.

> P: *Press into Jesus.* Don't run from your pain; run to the One who was wounded for you. He understands. He cares. He heals. Press into Jesus by reading, meditating on, and praying Scripture.
>
> A: *Acknowledge the hurt.* Denial delays healing. Name the pain so Jesus can redeem it.
>
> I: *Invite others into your healing journey.* Healing isn't a solo journey. Let the church be the hospital it was meant to be. Seek wise counsel that points you to Jesus and a caring community who loves you well. Invite a good therapist to help you.
>
> N: *Name your new life.* Jesus didn't just carry and forgive your sin. He carried your sorrow, too. When he rose from the dead, you rose to new life with new power.

If you're on the path of healing, remember that there will be turbulence. You're going to make it. Jesus is with you. He's flying you home and will not let you go.

Prayer

Father,
You are the Restorer of shattered stories.

Jesus,
You are flying me through the storm.
When I feel turbulence,
I will press into you.

Holy Spirit,
Help me trade the lies for truth.
And when it hurts more to heal than it did to be hurt,
remind me that I am not alone.

In your healing love,
amen.

Reflection Questions

1. What might change in your life if you chose to fly through the storm—doing the hard work of developing scar tissue over your wounds—instead of staying grounded in your pain?

   Acknowledge your fears. Write them down and draw a cross over them.

2. Are you willing to embrace the pain that heals so you can leave behind the pain that keeps wounding you and those you love?

Write down the acronym *PAIN.*

What does it look like for you to press into Jesus (**P**)?

What hurt do you need to acknowledge (**A**)?

Whom do you trust to invite (**I**) into your journey?

Who are you naming (**N**) your new life with? (Claim your new life in Christ. Tell yourself, *I have new life in Jesus.*)

CHAPTER 6

Evidence Is Your Friend

God is breaking through with a better story.

Icebergs fascinate me. These massive towers of freshwater ice break off from ancient glaciers and drift across the open sea. They look huge on the surface, but what we see is only a fraction of their true size. About 10 percent rises above the water. The other 90 percent is hidden out of sight. That's the heart behind the phrase *the tip of the iceberg*. The real mass, the real story, is quietly waiting beneath the waves.

People are the same way. We show the world 10 percent of ourselves, but the real story—our fears, insecurities, wounds, longings, and unhealed places—lives beneath the surface. And it's the beneath-the-surface part of us that motivates our thoughts, emotions, and behaviors.

God wants to meet us below the surface, in the hidden places we often avoid. Below the surface is where God does his important work of grace.

I want to show you three pictures from the life of a man whose story should have crumbled under the weight of everything hidden beneath the surface. Yet his life has become living proof that God can take the brokenness no one sees and turn it into strength that blesses the world.

Picture #1: The Slums of India

The first picture takes us deep into the Khalpar Slum in Kolkata, India, a community built on top of a garbage dump. The air is heavy with heat, and the poverty is severe. But somehow, in the middle of it all, hope lives.

In this place where the cruel Eastern philosophy of Karma teaches that suffering is punishment for sins in a past life, Jesus is breaking through with a better story. A powerful ministry led by faithful Indian brothers and sisters in Christ is thriving among these resilient people.[1] With sleeves rolled up, they are healing lives by meeting urgent physical and emotional needs. Children are being educated. Leaders are being developed. Job training is happening. Hope is rising.

There's a man in this picture. He was invited to step into the heart of the Khalpar Slum to serve and share the gospel at an outreach event. That night, as people filled the slum, the anticipation of hearing the gospel was electric. Under the sweltering sky, the slum became holy ground. Many people gave their lives to Jesus. Many traded Karma for God's grace.

But something else happened too. The preacher's life was changed. Watching his Indian brothers and sisters follow Jesus with joy and boldness in such hardship lit a fire in him.

Where the world sees garbage, God sees a garden of redemption.

As the man surveyed his life, he was shocked that he was preaching the gospel in Kolkata. He had stuttered for most of his life. He hadn't even grown up going to church. Preaching the gospel in India or anywhere was not even a dream he thought he could dream. But he met Jesus, the Healer. He learned that much of his stuttering was the result of childhood trauma. He had seen things no child should ever see. Because of the chaos and violence surrounding him, he had been a nervous, fearful child.

How could this man now be a preacher of the gospel?

Picture #2: Graduation

The second picture is quieter but sacred. A man stands in his doctoral robe, surrounded by his wife and two children. It's more than a photo. It's a testimony. He remembers the admiration in his wife's eyes and the love of his children as they looked at him that day. His wife knew how long and hard this road had been for him to travel. She knew he was one of the few men in his family to graduate from high school. She remembered when he had barely gotten into college with a 16 on his ACT. She remembered when he had nearly flunked out with a 1.41 GPA his first semester. She remembered reading books aloud to him because he hated reading; he'd said that when he read, the words jumped around the page.

But now she was holding the hand of a man in a cap and gown, holding a doctorate, because God had rewritten his story.

This moment wasn't just his victory. It was theirs. And it was holy.

How does a man earn a doctorate when, for most of his life, he believed he was incapable? He had been too afraid to raise his hand in class because when he spoke the other kids laughed. After eighth grade, he'd had no one at home to help him with his homework because no one in his family had gone beyond eighth grade. So how did he end up in a doctoral robe?

Picture #3: Wedding Anniversary

In the third picture, the man and his wife are celebrating thirty-four years of marriage. Their love story began when he was just eighteen and she was nineteen. They were young, broke college students when they stood at the altar. For his family, marriage wasn't common. In fact, getting married was so unfamiliar to him that the first wedding he attended was his own.

Thirty-four years later, through every high and every low, their love has not only survived; it has thrived. What began as a teenage romance has become a living testimony of God's grace. But where grace is needed, deep brokenness is present. Grace only flows into broken people.

At first, he carried insecurities he didn't know how to name. He didn't know how to resolve conflict, so he became a passive husband and father. His fear of emotional intimacy and abandonment kept him guarded, holding his wife at a distance even though he loved her. The emotional enmeshment of his family had left him unsure of how to set boundaries or even recognize his own need for boundaries. It had wounded his young wife. It had wounded him. And he'd had no idea how to fix it.

How has this man been married for thirty-four years when marriage wasn't modeled for him? How is he now a loving, present husband and father when his own father was not present?

The Evidence

The man in these three pictures is me.

Jesus stepped into my story like an artist stepping up to a ruined canvas. He took the ashes of abuse and started painting grace.

He took the wounds from my absent father and began filling them with forgiveness.

He gave me a love for learning and a curious mind.

The pain I've experienced is very real.

The evidence of Jesus' grace is even more real.

And friend, what he did for me, he can do for you. No matter where you come from, no matter what's been done to you or done by you, Jesus is greater.

With the power of the Holy Spirit, the steady love of my wife, godly mentors, and a bunch of books, I slowly began to believe in something better than my trauma. I started to trust what Jesus had accomplished *for me* more than what had been done *to me*.

I'm living what psychologists Richard Tedeschi and Lawrence Calhoun call posttraumatic growth (PTG).[2] PTG is the powerful truth that even after deep psychological struggle people can grow stronger, wiser, and more grounded because of what they've endured. Dr. Tedeschi says, "People develop new understandings of themselves, the world they live in, how to relate to other people, the kind of future they might have and a better understanding of how to live life."[3]

I share my story with you so you can see that God is able to do more than we can imagine.

The evidence of God's grace says that he takes the wreckage of our lives and forms something beautiful.

We are not our pasts.

We are God's masterpiece, recreated in Christ Jesus.

> We are God's masterpiece. He has created us anew in Christ Jesus, so we can do the good things he planned for us long ago.
>
> **EPHESIANS 2:10, NLT**

The Greek word *poiēma* here refers to God's workmanship, artwork, or masterpiece.

God the Artist recreates us as his living artwork of grace in Christ Jesus.

The evidence says we are God's masterpiece.

The cross is the final verdict, an unalterable fact in the fabric of the universe.

You are God's masterpiece.[4]

You are now more than what was done to you.

Your past wounds are not greater than Jesus.

Jesus speaks life over you.

You are his artwork, colored by his life-giving blood.

The paintbrush of God is recreating you.

Prayer

Father,
For too long I've hidden the 90 percent
beneath the surface.
I'm tired of pretending.
I'm ready for your love to reach the deep places
and heal me.

Jesus,
You step into my life the way an artist approaches
a ruined painting,
not to discard it but to restore it.
Today I open myself to you.
Paint over my insecurities, my trauma, my sin.
Let your blood cover me.
Heal me.

Holy Spirit,
Give me eyes of faith to see what the Father sees
when he looks at me—
his masterpiece, recreated in Christ.

Amen.

Reflection Questions

1. What if the pain of your past is not the end of your story but the beginning of your testimony?

Write down one piece of "evidence" from your past that you thought disqualified you. Then, by faith, write what Jesus is saying about it now. Let his truth rewrite the story.

2. What part of your life is still hiding beneath the surface, quietly shaping your thoughts and emotions? Are you willing to let God meet you there?

CHAPTER 7

Engage God's Grace in the Pain

The wilderness is a place of healing.

Every villain and every hero starts at the same place: pain. But what they do with it determines their destiny. A villain lets pain harden them. It blisters into bitterness, blame, and a thirst for control. Their wounds become weapons that hurt others.

A hero finds their origin in pain also, but they choose a different path. They let it humble, purify, and shape them. A hero's wounds become wisdom. Instead of spreading pain, they look to rescue others who are hurting.

Pain bends one person into the shape of a villain, and it molds another into a hero. It destroys one life and rebuilds another. In the end, it's not the pain that determines who we become. It's our response to the pain that writes the future chapters of our lives.

Let me tell you a story about a boy born into pain. His home was dominated by an emotionally and physically abusive father who ruled with control and intimidation. If the boy disobeyed, he was met with brutal beatings. His home was not a safe place to be a child. He also watched his mother be beaten by his father. At an early age, the lie that power always came with cruelty was seared into his consciousness.

While reading Karl May, a popular adventure novelist, he discovered one concept that gave him a sense of control: *The brave man gives no sign of being in pain.* The next time his father beat him, the boy met every blow with silence. Afterward, he told his mother, with twisted pride, "Father hit me thirty-two times . . . and I did not cry."

As the boy grew older, he poured his pain into his art. He applied to art school twice and was rejected both times. The rector told him he had no talent for painting. The rejection carved another scar into his already angry, frail heart.

The boy began to believe that he was destined for greatness but that the world was against him—that people kept denying him his place of prominence. His wounds metastasized into racial hatred. His friends started to notice that his life was unraveling.

He endured the trauma of war and returned from it full of resentment. Instead of healing, he fed his wounds with blame. Instead of seeking peace, he worshiped power. He came to believe that might makes right and that racial supremacy was the only path to his destiny.

That boy's name was Adolf Hitler.[1] His unresolved pain became fuel that led to the genocidal massacre of millions of Jews.

The world went to war because of an unhealed little boy who became a villain.

Millions died.

Another Story of Pain

Now let me tell you the story of another boy born into pain. He was from a country that was colonized and poisoned by racism, segregation, and injustice. He watched his people be stripped of their dignity simply because of the color of their skin. The pain of his fellow countrymen and his own personal pain caused him to pursue justice for all people. This pursuit cost him twenty-seven years of his life behind prison bars, many of those years spent in solitary confinement.

He was torn from his family.

He missed his children growing up.

He had every reason to let his pain become destructive and vengeful. Instead, the pain became a womb that nurtured love, compassion, and unshakable resolve.

When he was finally released from prison, he didn't call for riots or retribution; he called for peace, forgiveness, and reconciliation.

This little boy was Nelson Mandela.

With words shaped by years of suffering, he said, "I have fought against white domination, and I have fought against black domination. I have cherished the ideal of a democratic and free society in which all persons live together in harmony and with equal opportunities. It is an ideal which I hope to live for and to achieve. But if needs be, it is an ideal for which I am prepared to die."[2]

On May 10, 1994, the world watched this man, once branded a criminal, become South Africa's first democratically elected president. He could have become a tyrant, but he chose to become a healer.

His scars didn't make him cruel.

His scars made him courageous.

His wounds didn't lead to war but to the birth of a nation.

Mandela, a Methodist, once said, "I realized that they could take everything from me except my mind and my heart. They could not take those things. Those things I still had control over. And I decided not to give them away."[3]

Pain Is Not the End of the Story

In the beautiful mystery of Jesus infusing his life into ours, pain and trauma do not get the final word. Your response does.

Will you let belief in what happened to you be greater than faith in Jesus and what he has done to heal you?

You can let your wounds become weapons or wisdom.

You can let the fire devour you, or you can let it refine you.

Who you become in the fire is determined by what you let burn.

Let bitterness burn and you'll find healing.

Let hatred burn and you'll discover love.

And never forget, God is in the fire with you, calling you to trust him.

He's not distant.

He's not silent.

He's refining, sustaining, and transforming you.

God wants to form a hero in you. Please let him.

A Little Girl's Story

There's one more story I want to share with you. A little girl was born into a family of watchmakers. She grew up learning the rhythms of grace and the ways of Jesus in her Christian family. During World War II, her family became a beacon of courage by rescuing at-risk neighbors from the tyrannical regime that was invading their country.

She and thirty people in her home were arrested. Most of them were released, but she, her sister, and their father remained imprisoned. Her dad died in prison. Yet she and her sister clung to their faith even in inhumane concentration camp conditions.

After her release, she returned home, filled not with bitterness but with boldness to proclaim the gospel. She spent her days preaching and helping victims heal from their trauma.

This girl was Corrie ten Boom.[4] She used her pain to become a hero, not a villain.

A villain hurts those who hurt them.

Heroes forgive those who hurt them.

While preaching in Germany, Corrie was confronted by one of her cruel former prison guards. Here's how she describes this encounter:

It could not have been many seconds that he stood there—hand held out—but to me it seemed hours as

I wrestled with the most difficult thing I had ever had to do.

For I had to do it—I knew that. The message that God forgives has a prior condition: that we forgive those who have injured us. "If you do not forgive men their trespasses," Jesus says, "neither will your Father in heaven forgive your trespasses."

I knew it not only as a commandment of God, but as a daily experience. Since the end of the war, I had had a home in Holland for victims of Nazi brutality. Those who were able to forgive their former enemies were able also to return to the outside world and rebuild their lives, no matter what the physical scars. Those who nursed their bitterness remained invalids. It was as simple and as horrible as that.

And still I stood there with the coldness clutching my heart. But forgiveness is not an emotion—I knew that too. Forgiveness is an act of the will, and the will can function regardless of the temperature of the heart. *Jesus, help me!* I prayed silently. *I can lift my hand. I can do that much. You supply the feeling.*

And so woodenly, mechanically, I thrust my hand into the one stretched out to me. And as I did, an incredible thing took place. The current started in my shoulder, raced down my arm, sprang into our joined hands. And then this healing warmth seemed to flood my whole being, bringing tears to my eyes.

"I forgive you, brother!" I cried. "With all my heart."

For a long moment we grasped each other's hands, the former guard and the former prisoner. I had never known God's love so intensely as I did then. But even so, I realized it was not my love. I had tried, and did not have the power. It was the power of the Holy Spirit as recorded in Romans 5:5: " . . . because the love of God is shed abroad in our hearts by the Holy Ghost which is given unto us."[5]

Pain shaped Hitler into a tyrant.

Pain shaped Mandela into a liberator.

Pain shaped ten Boom into a healer.

You may never become the president of a nation or a world-renowned evangelist and justice seeker, but your healing can bless future generations in your family, friendships, and community.

We are all going to experience deep pain in this life. Jesus told us as much.[6]

Engage God's grace in the pain so he can transform you into a hero.

The Lord is near the brokenhearted;
he saves those crushed in spirit.

PSALM 34:18

Prayer

Father of mercy,
You see every wound.
You hear every silent cry.
You know the pain I carry.

Jesus,
You've seen what pain can do when it goes unhealed,
how it can twist hearts,
poison minds,
and multiply suffering.
But I know what pain can do when it is placed
in your hands,
how it can forge courage,
birth compassion,
and bring healing to a broken world.

Holy Spirit,
Turn my wounds into wisdom.
Turn my scars into strength.
Purify me in the fire.
Shape me in the struggle.

In the name of Jesus, who bore the ultimate pain
to bring us healing,
amen.

Reflection Questions

1. Will you let your pain harden you or heal you?

   When have you let pain harden you? What did that look like? What was the result?

2. What affected you most from Hilter's, Mandela's, and ten Boom's stories? Why?

CHAPTER 8

Enter Rest

"Come to me, all of you who are weary and burdened, and I will give you rest."

JESUS OF NAZARETH (MATTHEW 11:28)

I once heard it said that *BUSY* is an acronym for "Being Under Satan's Yoke." One of the most toxic traits of modern life is how we worship busyness. But we may not realize how, in our pain, we can use busyness to maintain the feeling of being in control or as an addictive drug to numb us. Hurried people can't feel the full weight of their wounds. But hurried people can't heal either.

We hustle.

We grind.

We chase overfunctioning like it's a badge of honor.

There's always more to do.

And all the while, we're distracting ourselves. We're running and performing and living in all the ways that keep us from hurting, even as our wounds are leaking from the inside out.

It's like we're having a slow-motion spiritual heart attack.

We're flooded with anxiety.

Drenched in depression.

We're lonely and isolated and frantic to pretend everything is okay.

Using the pace of our lives to avoid our pain keeps us in a constant state of cortisol overload. The resulting stress "can make us more vulnerable to disease, which is why many researchers now believe that toxic stress is responsible for up to approximately 90 percent of illness, including heart disease, cancer, and diabetes. Only 5-10 percent of disease is said to come from genetic factors alone."[1] But more than that—all this is killing us spiritually and physically.

When I was growing up, people used to say that life is a rat race. Here's the problem: You're not a rat, so why are you in a race for rats?

You are the beloved of the Father.

He didn't create you to live an unhealthy, hurried life.

He didn't create you to run yourself ragged so you can't feel your pain.

He created you to live a fruitful, productive, joyful life.

Our Father created us to live at the pace of grace, resting and relying on the Spirit's power.

> By the grace of God I am what I am, and his grace toward me was not in vain. On the contrary, I worked harder than any of them, yet not I, but the grace of God that was with me.
>
> **1 CORINTHIANS 15:10**

The Lies of Self-Sufficiency

From the beginning, the seductive liar has bombarded humanity with three lies that keep us from depending on God and healing from our brokenness.[2]

Lie #1: I Am What I Do

The lie of performance-based living tells you that your identity and worth are found in what you accomplish. *The more you achieve*, it whispers, *the more valuable you will feel*. If you fail, you feel worthless. Either way, it's idolatry. Your achievement is your god.

As we fall for this lie, we start believing that achievement can heal us. We think if we accomplish enough, succeed enough, or earn enough, the pain will finally ease. But no matter how much money I made in the NFL, no matter how grown I looked in the mirror, the insecure, helpless little boy still stared back at me. It's a painful moment when you realize you can never achieve your way into healing.

Lie #2: I Am What Others Think of Me

The lie of approval-based living tells us that our identity and worth are found in what other people think about us.

We think we'll feel whole if we can just get others' approval.

We pretend to be what others want us to be.

We morph into people pleasers so others will like us.

We build a version of ourselves that isn't real. And the gap between who we are and who we pretend to be becomes a deep, dark chasm. The wider the chasm, the harder the fall. We are exhausted from faking it. That, too, is idolatry.

When we believe the lie that pleasing people will fix the broken pieces of our hearts, we set ourselves up for even deeper hurt. We become easy to manipulate, quick to sacrifice our own well-being, and slow to name what we truly need. Instead of healing us, people pleasing only widens the wounds we're trying to hide. True healing begins when we stop chasing approval and start letting God tend to the aching places within us.

Lie #3: I Am What I Possess

The lie of possession-based living tells us that our identity and worth are found in what we accumulate. We have faith that our house, car, clothes, spouse, kids, and social media followers will satisfy us. But no matter how many things or followers we possess, it's never enough. Eventually, our possessions end up possessing us. We exhaust ourselves worrying about status, burning ourselves out to earn more money to buy more stuff that will not bring ultimate satisfaction. Then the anxiety of losing it all destroys us. This is idolatry. Eventually, we wake up to the truth that what we buy can't heal us. Only the love and wisdom of the God who bought us with his own blood can reach the places that ache and make us whole again.

The Freedom of Grace

All our lives we're taught to be self-reliant. *Try harder. Do more. Be better.* And if you grow up with critical, judgmental parents, that message gets written deep into your soul. Without even knowing it, we start carrying that same mindset into our relationship with Jesus. We imagine him saying, "I did my part. Now you do yours."

But that's not the gospel. Not even close.

The gospel says that Jesus does it all. He doesn't ask us to perform for him. He asks us to trust him. The gospel is good news for people who know they can't fix themselves. Grace is for the poor in spirit, the ones honest enough to say, "I need someone greater than me to save every part of me."

And that's where my healing journey began. I realized it could be summed up like this:

Jesus gave his life for you,
to give his life to you,
so he could live his life through you.
Jesus is the remedy for your weary soul.

The apostle Paul says it this way:

> I have been crucified with Christ, and I no longer live, but Christ lives in me. The life I now live in the body, I live by faith in the Son of God, who loved me and gave himself for me.
>
> **GALATIANS 2:20**

Jesus is your Core Reactor, who empowers you to overcome the three lies of the liar.

Lie #1: You Are What You Do (Performance-Based Living)

After Jesus fasted for forty days in the wilderness, the liar said to him, "If you are the Son of God, tell these stones to become bread."[3] This was a trap. The dark power was baiting

Jesus to abandon the Father's love and fall into performance-based living.

He was telling Jesus to prove himself by doing his own will instead of the Father's will.

But Jesus didn't take the bait, because he came to do his Father's will, not his own. He didn't strive to prove his worth because he already knew his worth. At Jesus' baptism, the Father had declared:

> "This is my beloved Son, with whom I am
> well-pleased."
>
> **MATTHEW 3:17**

As Satan tempted him, Jesus anchored himself in the Word of God: "It is written: Man must not live on bread alone but on every word that comes from the mouth of God."[4] Jesus didn't perform to discover his identity, because he knew his identity—his Father's beloved Son.

We often suffer more in our minds than in our circumstances. We start believing the lie that we are what we do. But when is performance-based living enough? Never. And that's how we get trapped in a loop of lies. We rehearse them over and over, and the more we do, the bigger our wounds feel, and the smaller our hope becomes. But when we root ourselves in our belovedness, something shifts. The love of God begins to flow into the hurt places and remind us that we are not what we fear, not what we've done, and not what was done to us. We are who God says we are—his beloved. That truth lifts our eyes off ourselves and onto the God who heals. And when his love touches the wounds we've been hiding, healing finally begins to form us, over time, into whole, healthy people.

Lie #2: You Are What Others Think of You (Approval-Based Living)

Next, the liar took Jesus to the highest point of the Jewish Temple in Jerusalem and dared him, *If you are the Son of God, throw yourself down, and the angels will catch you.*[5] The liar was tempting Jesus to build his life on what others thought of him.

He was saying, *Jesus, show the world who you are.*

Jesus, win their praise.

Let the people know who you are.

This was tempting because at this point in his life Jesus hadn't performed a single miracle.

To most people, he was just Joseph's son from Nazareth. He was a nobody from a nowhere town.[6] If Jesus jumped and angels caught him in midair, everyone would finally see him for who he really was.

But Jesus didn't live for the applause of people, because he knew the cheers of his Father. His identity and worth were found in the Father's love, not the opinions of fickle humans.

Once again, Jesus slapped the liar in the face with God's Word: "Do not test the Lord your God."[7] God's Word is truer than every lie the enemy whispers. The more we tune our ears to what God has spoken, the easier it becomes to silence the voices that try to deceive us. His truth is not just information—it's medicine for the soul. His Word heals, steadies, and strengthens us.

Lie #3: You Are What You Possess (Possession-Based Living)

Finally, the liar appealed to the idol of possessions. "The devil took [Jesus] to a very high mountain and showed him all the kingdoms of the world and their splendor. And he said to him, 'I will give you all these things if you will fall down and worship me.'"[8] Imagine the arrogance. Satan offered the Creator what already belonged to him! And still, he offers us the same hollow promise:

- *If you had more money, you'd be somebody.*
- *If you had a bigger house, you'd be somebody.*
- *If you had more expensive, name-brand clothes, you'd be somebody.*
- *If you had more power, you'd be somebody.*
- *If you just had more, then you'd matter.*

Corporations spend billions upon billions of dollars per year deceiving and seducing us to believe the lies.

Jesus did not take the liar's bait. He said, "Go away, Satan! For it is written: Worship the Lord your God, and serve only him."[9]

Jesus knew that his identity and worth didn't come from owning the world. They came from being loved by his Father. In my healing journey, this truth has helped me more than anything: *How valuable must I be to God if he chose to purchase me?* The greatest treasure in the universe, King Jesus, bought me with his life. With all my faults, all my triggers and traumas, and all my sins, he loved me enough to make me his own when I had nothing to offer him. He simply loved me because he wanted to love me.

When I sit with that truth, healing starts to rise in me. It burns away the lie that I am what I own. It reminds me that I am bought and cherished by God. And because of that, I carry an inherited worth beyond anything I could ever imagine.

Pull Up the Roots

Let's pull the lies up by the roots:

Who are you?

- *You are what Christ has done.* (Christ Performance–Based Living)

  You are loved beyond comprehension, completely forgiven, and declared eternally righteous.

  There's nothing left to prove.

  Jesus did it all for you.

  The cross was enough.

  Now you can breathe, rest, and live securely in his inseparable love.
- *You are who God says you are.* (Christ Approval–Based Living)

  You are God's masterpiece, crafted by grace, shaped by mercy, and filled with the Spirit, with nothing to prove to anyone.
- *You are his possession.* (Christ Possession–Based Living)

  You belong to the One who formed you, fought for you, and bled for you. You are his holy residence.

God loves loving you.

He delights in lavishing his grace on you.

With a smile on his face, he loves to reach down and pick his kids up so they can rest in his unfathomable, unending, life-giving grace.

> He chose us in him, before the foundation of the world, to be holy and blameless in love before him. He predestined us to be adopted as sons through Jesus Christ for himself, according to the good pleasure of his will, to the praise of his glorious grace that he lavished on us in the Beloved One.
>
> **EPHESIANS 1:4-6**

Today, and every day, you have a choice. By faith, you can believe the words God has spoken over you in Christ, words sealed into your very being by the Holy Spirit. Or you can listen to the lies of the enemy, who wants to keep you wounded and afraid.

Choose the voice of the One who calls you beloved.

Choose the voice of the One who purchased you with his own blood.

Choose the voice of the One called *Jehovah Rapha*.

By faith, refuse to listen to the lies that try to hold you back from healing.

Lean into the Father's voice of grace.

He is calling your name.

Prayer

Father,
Thank you that I am not what I do,
not what others think of me,
and not what I possess.
Thank you that healing begins with knowing
who I am in you.

Jesus,
Remind me daily that I am the Father's beloved,
his treasured child.
Heal the places in me that still believe the lies.
Rewire my mind with your Word.

Holy Spirit,
Root me in your grace.
Recenter my soul in your presence.
Do your healing work deep within me.
I am yours.
And that is enough.

In Jesus' name,
amen.

Reflection Questions

1. Have you believed the lies that your value comes from what you do or what others think about you or what you own?

Write down the three biggest lies you've believed about your identity.

- *I am what I do.*
- *I am what others think of me.*
- *I am what I possess.*

Why have you believed these lies?

How has believing these lies kept you from facing your wounds and finding healing in Christ?

2. Now, beside each lie, write the truth of who you are in Christ.

   Post these truths somewhere visible as a daily reminder that God's grace is sufficient as you face your pain and heal in his love.

COUNSELORS' CORNER

Rest

VICKEY MACLIN (PsyD, LPA)

Many people come to counseling exhausted from life's painful difficulties. Rest is nonexistent. Some have had stressors for so long that by the time they choose to enter counseling they hope the counselor will offer answers and healing. They are disappointed to learn that the counselor becomes the person who journeys in helping lead them toward rest.

In my clinical work, I have found that the three lies explained in this chapter can result in deeper levels of exhaustion. The first lie, *I am what I do*, leads to anxiety and to pain about being a failure. The second lie, *I am what others think of me*, can cause a constant striving to be accepted, resulting in insecurity and anxiety. The lie *I am what I possess* can lead people to feel as if they are not enough, resulting in depression.

When folks engage in these ways of thinking, the effect is exhaustion. My recommendation is to learn to be comfortable with who you are, not with what others say about who you are or even with what you say about yourself. Either way of living is often based on lies. Instead, challenge the lies. Seek evidence of what is true and relinquish holding on to the lie, which only increases stress, anxiety, and depression. A practical way to consider this, whether you are a Christ follower or not, is to think of the movie *Up* and consider what you need to throw out so that you can begin to soar.[10]

PART 3

A: *Accepting What Happened to You*

Acceptance is not approval. It's refusing to let your past hold the pen that writes your future.

CHAPTER 9

Awaken to What God Is Doing

You have to own your trauma,
or your trauma will own you.
DETECTIVE FIN TUTUOLA

Imagine discovering that your birth certificate didn't have your name on it, just the word *Unwanted*. No identity. No belonging. Just abandonment.

We usually reserve the word *unwanted* for things, not people. An old shirt. Spoiled milk. A piece of junk mail. But what if *unwanted* was the first word spoken over your life?

Experiencing abandonment isn't just a moment; it's a wound that has the potential to yell every day, "You're not worth it." As therapist Andrea Mathews writes, "The adult who was an unwanted child may, therefore, have a great deal of difficulty believing that he is loved. . . . There may also be a great deal of insecurity or even fear about performing in the world."[1]

Often, unwanted people do unhealthy things to feel wanted. Some people-please to the detriment of their own health. Some give their bodies away, hoping sex will feel like belonging. Others lie, cheat, or steal to try to gain acceptance.

If someone only wants you when you're toxic, they don't want you. They want to use you. And when they're done with you, you'll feel emptier than before.

Only God wants you with pure, beautiful motives. God doesn't want anything from you. God wants something *for* you: healing.

When the world uses and abuses us, we can speak this truth over ourselves: "Even if my father and mother abandon me, the Lord cares for me."[2]

God sees your mess. He knows and enters your pain. And he says,

- *You are mine.*
- *You are wanted.*
- *You are loved.*

You are like a precious coin that has been lost. God searches for you.

You are like a lost lamb. He leaves the ninety-nine to find you.

People may not want you, but God does. God wants unwanted people.

> "This is what the Lord God says: See, I myself will search for my flock and look for them. As a shepherd looks for his sheep on the day he is among his scattered flock, so I will look for my flock. I will

rescue them from all the places where they have been scattered on a day of clouds and total darkness."

EZEKIEL 34:11-12

Scene #1: Suffering in Shame

There once was a girl with *Unwanted* on her birth certificate. The name followed her as she grew up. Throughout her childhood, she was abused by several different men. She tried to tell someone. But back then, people didn't talk about that kind of stuff. They looked away. They stayed silent. The trauma piled on, layer after layer, until it crushed her. She felt abandoned. Unsafe. Unseen. Unwanted. Unloved. Damaged.

Years of silent suffering filled her with anger, guilt, and shame.

Guilt tells you, *I did something wrong.*

Shame gossips to your soul, *I* am *what's wrong.*

For years, I blamed my six-year-old self for playing hide-and-seek with a teenager in the woods behind the apartment complex where I lived with my mom. I told myself that I had caused what happened. That I should've known better. But how could I have known better? I was six. What happened wasn't my fault. And I am not what happened to me.

It took meeting Jesus on August 2, 1997, for that truth to break through and free me from shame. Until then, I had buried my pain behind a football helmet and uniform. I was NFL strong. But even success couldn't hide the wound. That hidden pain showed up in my insecurity, my fear, and a soul that never felt safe.

God doesn't usually heal what we don't reveal. Before the healing journey can begin, we must tell the truth and accept what happened. I don't know what your "what happened" is, but God does. We must bring our real selves to the feet of Jesus. And when we do, we don't find a distant God. We find a God with tears in his eyes, saying, *I saw it. I hated it. I suffered with you. I'm here to heal you.*

As we mourn the harm that was done to us, we're also facing the painful truth that it really did happen. We're not denying it anymore. Our hearts begin to feel what our minds have tried to forget. In this sacred and honest place of grief, healing sprouts.

Jesus said, "Blessed are those who mourn, for they will be comforted."[3]

So cry.

Grieve what was stolen.

Be angry.

But don't let someone else's sin cause you to sin.

Every tear you cry is caught and bottled by God. In his hands, tears become healing rain.

Graveyards of shame become gardens of grace.

Scene #2: Encountering the Healer

Through the compassion of a loving friend and the bold preaching of an evangelist, the girl who believed she was unwanted encountered the saving love of God in Christ Jesus. As she beheld the cross, the eyes of her heart opened to how much God wanted her.

She discovered that even in the darkest moments of her life, God had been with her.

He had cried with her.

He had always cared.

He had always wanted her.

At the cross, the God who bled and died didn't just suffer *for* her—he suffered *with* her.

Jesus isn't a distant deity. He has skin in the game. Better yet, he has blood in the game. He is the Suffering Servant, who came to heal our hearts and cleanse us of all unrighteousness. That's what he did for the girl born with the name *Unwanted.* The wounds those men had left behind began to be healed through the deeper wounds in Christ's own body.

As she abandoned herself to Jesus, she was reborn.

A new heart replaced her old one.

The Holy Spirit took residence.

She was no longer an orphan.

She became Abba's girl.

The same is true for you. When you let the Holy Spirit carry you to the cross of Christ, the unsearchable, unconquerable riches of Christ transfer you from the kingdom of darkness into the Kingdom of light.[4]

You are given a brand-new identity: adopted.

You stand in a new position: partaker in the divine nature.

You are in Christ. Nothing can separate you from his life.

This is why the gospel is epic.

God the Father signed the adoption papers in the blood of Jesus.

And the Spirit seals you to him forever.

If this is true—and it is—

- Why do we still feel so much guilt and shame?
- Why do our hearts still ache like we're alone?
- Why do we keep chasing love in places that only leave us empty and wounded?
- Why do we still believe we're unwanted?

The apostle Paul wrestled with this tension too. He wrote, "I do not understand what I am doing, because I do not practice what I want to do, but I do what I hate."[5]

This tension has a name: sanctification. Sanctification is the Spirit-empowered journey of becoming in *practice* who you already are by *position*.

Our Position in Christ	Our Practice in Christ
fully forgiven (Colossians 2:13)	We forgive others. (Ephesians 4:32)
declared righteous (2 Corinthians 5:21)	We pursue righteous living. (1 Peter 1:15-16)
loved unconditionally (Romans 8:38-39)	We love others sacrificially. (John 13:34-35)
seated with Christ (Ephesians 2:6)	We serve with humility. (Philippians 2:3-5)
a new creation (2 Corinthians 5:17)	We put off the old self. (Ephesians 4:22-24)

Our Position in Christ	**Our Practice in Christ**
adopted as children of God (Romans 8:15-17)	We walk in obedience as sons and daughters. (1 John 2:6)
set free from sin's power (Romans 6:6-7)	We say no to sin and yes to the Spirit. (Galatians 5:16)
secure in Christ (John 10:28-29)	We persevere in faith and love. (Hebrews 10:23-24)
filled with the Holy Spirit (Ephesians 1:13-14)	We bear the fruit of the Spirit. (Galatians 5:22-23)
called to holiness (1 Thessalonians 4:7)	We live holy lives in the world. (Romans 12:1-2)

In this beautiful yet painful tension

We daily commune with the Father.

We daily remind ourselves of who we are in Christ.

We daily delight in his love, and we invite the Holy Spirit into every thought, every emotion, every wound.

And slowly (sometimes painfully slowly) who we are in position becomes who we are in practice. That's why healing doesn't happen in isolation. We need wise people. Skilled people. Compassionate people. Gospel-saturated people to shepherd our hearts.

A wounded healer named Henri Nouwen wrote, "It is the Incarnate Christ who sends his Spirit. Therefore, it remains true that the Spirit of God reveals itself in the continuing incarnation of God in human history. Doctors, psychologists, therapists, all can be part of this continuing incarnation and so the instrument of God's Spirit."[6]

Don't be afraid to see a therapist. Let these soul physicians help you unearth what you've buried. Don't walk alone. Surround yourself with gospel-preaching, grace-filled people in a local church. Let the Word of God saturate your mind.

Abandon yourself to the Healer. And pray with each breath you take.

Sometimes God heals instantly. But more often, healing is a long journey of God "heal[ing] the brokenhearted and bandag[ing] [our] wounds."[7] So keep walking with Jesus, even if you have a limp. Keep going. Keep trusting. Your wounds are not the end of your story. Grace is.

Scene #3: Wounded Healer

The little girl who walked through hell is now a woman who has led hundreds of thousands toward the new heaven and new earth. The baby girl abandoned at birth is now one of the most powerful preachers of our generation. Her name is Christine Caine.

She's a fiery preacher, a global Christian leader, and a relentless hope bringer to some of the darkest places on earth. The power in Christine's preaching was born in the furnace of her pain. The soil of her deepest pain became the very ground where God planted the seeds of her calling. For decades now, she and her husband, Nick, have circled the globe strengthening the church, equipping leaders, and preaching Jesus with holy fire.

And in 2008, they launched A21, one of the largest anti–human trafficking organizations in the world. Nick and Christine, along with their global A21 team, are on the front lines breaking the cycle of human trafficking.[8] They've also planted churches in Bulgaria, Poland, and Greece. Through Propel Women, Christine is raising up generations of women to lead with both boldness and brilliance in ministry and the academy.

I once heard her say, "Sometimes when you're in a dark place, you think you've been buried. But really you've been planted."

My friend, the enemy thought he was burying you in a barren, dirty field of shame and self-pity. But what he didn't realize was that God was planting you. Rise in resurrection power.

> *God is able to take the mess of our past and turn it into a message. He takes the trials and tests and turns them into a testimony.*[9]
>
> **CHRISTINE CAINE**

Prayer

Father,
I bring you my buried wounds,
my silent screams,
and the tears I've cried when no one was watching.

Jesus,
You are the Suffering Servant.
You were wounded so we could be healed.

Holy Spirit,
Help me believe again.
Help me trust again.
And when I feel buried,
remind me that I've been planted so I can bloom.

In Jesus' name,
amen.

Reflection Questions

1. How does Christine Caine's statement that "sometimes when you're in a dark place, you think you've been buried. But really you've been planted" affect you?

   Write the names of three people who need to hear these words. Send each of them a message that includes this truth.

2. How does the truth that God wants you change the story of who you are?

   What step will you take because of being wanted by God?

   Take a step toward healing. Each morning this week, declare out loud, "I am wanted. I am loved. I am God's child."

CHAPTER 10

Address the Hurt

What you don't forgive, you relive.

The first time I met my father-in-law, he flew his Cessna 182 down from Hamilton, Montana, to Provo, Utah, where Vicki and I were students at Brigham Young University. I was eighteen. She was nineteen. We had only been dating for a few months, but she wanted me to meet her parents.

Dick walked up, extended his hand, and gave me a firm handshake. Imagine that John Wayne and Johnny Cash had their DNA spliced into one person. That's what Dick looked like—tough, rugged. I squeezed back with all the strength I had. I wanted him to know I was tough too. But I was totally intimidated, even though this first meeting went well. We ate dinner together and played volleyball.

About eighteen months later, Vicki and I got engaged and then married while we were still in college. Dick was never outwardly rude, never disrespectful—but I felt in my gut that he didn't want his White daughter to marry a Black man. Vicki later told me he had attempted to talk her out of marrying me. As you might expect, I was mad.

But over time, I started to understand Dick.

Every person has an origin story. And even if we may not realize it, most of those stories include some kind of trauma. In the 1950s, when Dick served in the Army, he was in a barrack full of White soldiers except for one Black soldier. When the Black soldier was picked on, Dick defended him. Later, Dick and that same soldier were moved to an all-Black barrack. When a few of the Black soldiers started to pick on Dick, his Black friend didn't stand up for him. That hurt him. It left a scar.

In my early twenties, I didn't care what Dick thought about me. If he didn't like me, so be it. I wasn't trying to win him over. But then something beautiful happened. Vicki and I met Jesus in the late 1990s, and our hearts changed toward Dick. Instead of staying angry at how he viewed me, we started praying for him to meet Jesus. If Jesus could change our hearts toward him, he could change Dick's heart toward me.

In 2001, while we were vacationing at Disney World, Vicki said, "I don't know how much longer we'll have with Dad. He needs to know Jesus." She came up with a wild idea: We were going to lock him and her mom in their hotel room and share the gospel with them. So we did.

We sat them down. Vicki dropped onto her knees, started crying, and shared the gospel with her dad. She told him about grace. About forgiveness. About eternal life.

God healed wounds that day. Both of Vicki's parents surrendered to Jesus, and a new relationship with my in-laws began.

A couple of years later, Dick had just come through cancer surgery when we all met up at a family reunion in Oregon. He pulled me into his RV and, with tears in his eyes, said, "Son, would you forgive me? I was wrong. You're a good man. You love my daughter." It was a holy moment. I had already forgiven him—because Jesus had already forgiven me. Who was I to withhold the very grace I'd been given?

After what I call the "RV Moment," Dick and I became best friends.

We golfed together.

We traveled together.

We laughed until we cried together.

Dad told the best stories. I hung on every single word!

When his friends came over to his house, he would proudly introduce me: "This is my son. He's a pastor."

And when he got too sick to golf, we just sat on the couch together.

We talked about eternal life.

We talked about death.

We talked about regrets.

We talked about all the laughs we'd had golfing.

Dad passed over a decade ago now. And I miss him. I miss our golf trips. I miss his Montana stories. I miss watching him sing and play guitar.

I miss my friend.

I miss my dad.

But I know I'll see him again.

The next time I see him, he will not be worn down from kidney failure and multiple heart attacks. He will be in a glorified, resurrected body. And you best believe we will golf again.

Change Is a Choice

Healing is never passive. It's always an active, vulnerable yes to God. Healing begins when we stop staring at the rearview mirror of our lives and dare to believe we are the beloved. My dad chose that path. He partnered with the Holy Spirit and moved forward.

I had the privilege of watching grace remake him from the inside out. In his journey, he showed us three powerful steps toward real and lasting change:

1. *Face the sin.* You can't heal what you won't face. Dick confessed to God that his prejudice was wrong. Then he confessed it to me. This is called repentance. Repentance is God inviting you to be healed. It's Jesus saying, *Turn around. Come home. I've already paid the price.* Scripture says, "If we confess our sins, he is faithful and righteous to forgive us our sins and to cleanse us from all unrighteousness."[1]

   God is faithful.
   God is righteous.
   God forgives.
   God cleanses.
   Grace calls us to turn to God, agreeing with him

that what we did was wrong. Repentance is a posture of humility that opens the door to deep, lasting healing.

Repentance is beautiful.

It's where shame dies.

It's where tears become joy.

It's where the past no longer has the final word over our lives—Jesus does.

Unhealed wounds don't heal on their own. They don't heal with time. Our wounds become weapons that wound others if we are not intentional about healing.

Dick's unhealed pain hurt me. It hurt his daughter. Old wounds don't stay dormant. They creep and crawl and bite. They trap us in patterns of sin. They shape how we see God, ourselves, and others. But God can break the cycle. When we run to him in repentance, he meets us with mercy. Jesus is God's Mercy Seat. And his mercy never runs out.

King David says it like this: "Be gracious to me, God, according to your faithful love; according to your abundant compassion, blot out my rebellion. Completely wash away my guilt and cleanse me from my sin. . . . The sacrifice pleasing to God is a broken spirit. You will not despise a broken and humbled heart, God."[2]

Repentance is a gift of grace. It stops wounds from turning into weapons.

2. *Learn to forgive.* Dick needed to experience God's grace to be able to forgive the Black soldiers who had mistreated him during his time in the military. For over forty years, he let the scar they left on him in 1953 bleed into his life. And it bled into my life in 1993. Dick projected and transferred his past pain onto me.

   If we're honest, we'll admit we've all done the same thing. We've hurt people because of the wounds someone else has given us. It's as if we bleed on people who haven't cut us.

   What you don't forgive, you relive. Dick was reliving his pain in his relationship with me. When we hold on to unforgiveness, we ruminate on how we were wronged. We replay the hurt repeatedly in our minds. We dig trenches of pain in our brains. Research shows that rumination can persist for years, even decades.[3]

   But our forgiving God taught Dick how to forgive. And friend, forgiveness is for *your* wounded heart. It breaks you free from the mental prison that someone else locked you in. Forgiveness is the key that opens the door to healing. The apostle Paul says it this way: "Be kind and compassionate to one another, forgiving one another, just as God also forgave you in Christ."[4]

3. *See with God's eyes.* As he repented and extended grace, Dick learned to see me the way God sees

> me. Instead of seeing me through a 1953 wound, he started seeing me through the blood of Jesus. He saw me as I truly was, as God's beloved son in Christ. He saw me as a man who loved Jesus more than anything in the world. A man who treasured his daughter and loved his grandchildren. He saw me grow from an eighteen-year-old kid into a man. And I saw him grow too. I guess you could say we grew up together.

What past hurts are hijacking your current relationships? And what faith-filled step is God inviting you to take toward healing?

Have you turned to Jesus in repentance? He's not waiting to punish you. He's waiting to heal you. Repentance is the first step toward freedom.

Is there a relationship you need to repair? A wound you need to stop ignoring? God's grace is big enough to redeem your story.

Don't wait.

Let grace do its work in you.

Dad's Going-Home Party

Dad and I would sit and talk late at night under the wide-open Montana sky, surrounded by the quiet canvas of stars. We had deep conversations about life, about God, about eternity. We laughed. We talked about the future he was about to step into. Dick knew his time was coming. And more than once, he looked at me and said, "Son, when it's time, I want you and Vicki to preach at my funeral. I love hearing you preach. Will you do that for me?"

When that day came, when it was time to celebrate his life, Dick's daughter, the little girl who once held on to his back while he cruised the open road on his motorcycle, and his Black son-in-law, the one he hadn't been sure about at first, stood together and preached the house down. We proclaimed the Good News of King Jesus, the One who defeated sin and death, the One who heals families, raises the dead, and is making all things new.

I pictured Dad with guitar in hand, hair slicked back like Johnny Cash, smiling, strumming, maybe even singing "Amazing Grace" as we preached.

See you later, Dad. I'll catch you on the back nine.

Prayer

Father,
Thank you that no heart is too hard,
no wound is too deep,
for your grace to reach.

Jesus,
Thank you for the beauty of repentance.
Thank you for forgiveness that breaks us free
from past hurts.
You turn scars into stories of grace.

Holy Spirit,
Help me see people through the eyes of Jesus.
Help me forgive like Jesus forgave me.
Until I see my loved ones again, I live in hope.
Because I know the story isn't over.
You are making all things new.

In Jesus' name,
amen.

Reflection Questions

1. What is an old wound you've been living with? Maybe it's betrayal, abandonment, or rejection. How might you be transferring that wound onto someone else just like Dick did?

Take five minutes today and ask the Holy Spirit, *Who have I been wounding because I haven't let you heal me?* Write down that person's name. Then ask God to begin healing that wound in you so you can stop the pattern and start a new legacy.

2. Who do you need to forgive so you can stop reliving the pain?

   Right now, name the person or event you haven't forgiven. Say out loud, "Jesus, I choose to forgive them because you have forgiven me." You may have to say it again tomorrow. And the day after. But each time, you're taking one more step toward freedom.

COUNSELORS' CORNER

Cancel the Debt

JIM CRESS (MA, LPC, CSAT, CMAT)

When I don't forgive someone who has hurt me, whether long ago or recently, I am at risk of taking a toxic journey of resentment. Resentment is like drinking poison but expecting the person who hurt you to get sick from it. When I ponder one of the New Testament words for forgiveness, *aphiēmi*, I gain a clearer, richer understanding of the practice. This form of forgiveness carries the meaning of canceling the debts of what has been done to you.

I invite you to find a safe, quiet place, maybe with a trusted Christian counselor, and list (1) the facts of what someone has done to hurt you and (2) the specific ways these facts harmed you. Is the effect of what has harmed you a five-dollar debt or a five-million-dollar debt?

Forgiving someone is both a decision and a process. Research finds that emotional or realized forgiveness typically takes time to catch up with the clear, decisive choice you have made to cancel the debts of how you have been harmed by someone. Often, the feeling of truly forgiving someone follows the choice to forgive them.

When you forgive someone who has hurt you, it is not primarily for the other person. When you cancel the debts of the harm or betrayal you have experienced, you free yourself from the bondage of letting the painful past influence your potential future.

CHAPTER 11

Advance Through the Scar Tissue

Your scars don't have to define you,
but they can refine you.

Every scar has a story. And this one is Kate's.[1]

Kate had a great plan. After college at Appalachian State University, she was going to spend ten months in Kazakhstan, a place that had captured her heart during two unforgettable summers. She loved the people. She loved the land. And more than anything, she loved introducing curious hearts to Jesus.

But the severe pain in her hip was working against her plan. As a former soccer player, Kate knew how to play through pain. You push through. You grit your teeth. You keep going. That's what she'd done for years with the hip pain that never seemed to go away. But entering her senior year, the pain was no longer whispering. It was screaming. Her mom begged her to see a doctor. And finally, she did.

The diagnosis shattered her plans. Kate had a condition called acetabular retroversion. Her hip sockets were rotated backward, causing the bones to tear at the soft lining every time she moved. The only solution was a brutal surgery called a periacetabular osteotomy. The surgeon would have to break her pelvis in three places, rotate it twenty degrees, and bolt it all back together with screws.

Kate's body and dream were broken. She sensed strongly that she would not return to Kazakhstan. She just couldn't physically handle it. Kate was devastated.

The doctor told her it would take nine months to heal from the surgery. She would even have to learn how to walk again. Then came another crushing blow. Kate wouldn't be able to fulfill her commitment to do a campus ministry internship. She couldn't even walk, let alone lead students or raise financial support. With a heavy heart, she told her ministry leaders she wouldn't be returning. She needed to heal.

Instead of being met with compassion, she experienced pressure. "We don't want to guilt you," they said, "but we really need you to come back." Not only was Kate's hip broken; trust with these ministry leaders was broken too. Disappointment flooded in like a wave she couldn't stop. Kate felt like a failure. She began to question her calling. Was she really made for ministry? Was her faith even strong enough?

As a tender college student chasing Jesus with everything she had, Kate felt like everything was being stripped away: Kazakhstan, the internship, her leaders' trust, and faith in her calling. In this grief, she discovered a hard truth: Her identity had been wrapped up more in what she did for Jesus than in what Jesus had done for her. Kate was trying to earn points with God to hear his praise instead of praising Jesus for earning her salvation.

After the surgery, Kate's hip bore a twelve-inch scar. But her soul bore scars too. She had to walk through soul rehab alongside physical rehab. Slowly. Painfully. Yet not alone. Through doctors, family, friends, and pastors, God the Holy Spirit walked on this journey with her. Little by little. Step by step. Kate began to heal both her hip and her heart.

Kate was a rock star on the Transformation Church production team for eight years. She leads with heart. She lights up rooms with her joy. Her spoken word pieces bring healing to others. Her hip still holds the twelve-inch scar that tells a story of victory.

Kate once told me, "It's worth remembering that God doesn't rescue us just to leave us where we were. And he doesn't allow painful chapters to be written for us to forget them. When we're broken, it's not because God is cruel; it's because he's rebuilding us into what we were always meant to be. God doesn't just repair you. He recreates you. You are his masterpiece."

SCAR

As we learn to move forward through the scars of life, it won't always be easy. Some days the healing journey will feel so heavy you'll want to quit. But in those moments, lift your eyes.

Remember who walks with you.

Remember that Jesus is with you.

He is your strength.

He is your endurance.

God took Kate's scars, seen and unseen, and turned them into a message of courage. And he can do the same for you. Through God's power and healing mercy, every SCAR can tell a story of healing.

S: *Surrender to God's Healing*

I'm sorry you're going through what you're going through. I'm sorry about what happened to you. Like the rest of humanity, you have scars, visible and invisible. Your twelve-inch scar may be a divorce, a parent's rejection, a friend's betrayal, or a past regret. Whatever it is, surrender it to the Healer.

In my early forties, I had to face a scar I had tried to ignore for years. I had buried the pain, but it had never really left me. It hid beneath the surface, affecting me more than I realized. The Holy Spirit began to nudge me, inviting me into deeper healing. It was hard. I had to look back at the pain from my upbringing.

I had to name it.

Feel it.

Grieve it.

Because what we don't grieve will not leave.

There were moments when healing felt too hard. But I knew I had to hand God the broken pieces of my heart. Being honest about the way things were didn't mean I don't love my family of origin. I do. But it did mean I had to advance through the scar tissue. I had to grieve it and leave it at the foot of the cross, where Jesus could take it. This is not a one-time act, but a lifelong holy habit.

Healing doesn't start when you try harder. It begins when you lay it all down.

C: *Cultivate Healing Community*

When hunting, a pride of lions does not attack a herd of their prey head on. They're strategic. They stalk. They know that strength is in their sheer numbers. Their goal isn't just to chase the herd; it's to cause panic and confusion. And in the chaos, the young, the weak, the injured, and those who lag get separated. And once they're alone, the lions pounce.

That's how the enemy works too. The Bible says in 1 Peter 5:8, "Your adversary the devil is prowling around like a roaring lion, looking for anyone he can devour." The enemy's strategy hasn't changed: divide and conquer. If he can separate you from the herd, if he can isolate you in your pain, shame, or pride, he can take you down. That's why believers run in packs. Isolation is the enemy's playground, but community is God's fortress.

You weren't meant to walk through pain alone. You need good mentors, friends, therapists, and pastors who can carry you to the throne of God's grace and mercy. God does his best soul rehab in community.

Who are you inviting to walk with you?

A: *Accept the Process*

One of the most painful lessons I learned in my professional football career is that if you come back too soon from an injury, you'll make the injury worse. In the 1996 playoffs with the Indianapolis Colts, I was dealing with a high ankle sprain. This type of injury usually takes at least six to eight weeks to heal.

I was only five weeks into rehab, but I was desperate to play against the Pittsburgh Steelers. So I pushed myself. I masked the pain. And as a veteran football player, I knew how to practice just well enough to convince the trainers and coaches that I was ready. Truth is, I wasn't. But I let pride blind me. I played. I was hurting. I ran with a limp. I didn't help the team that day. Someone else should have taken my place. And my injury got worse.

We do the same thing spiritually. Our souls get injured by trauma and sin, and instead of recovering, we rush the healing process. We fake it. We smile through the limp. We perform in church, in our relationships, at work . . . and the whole time, we're still bleeding inside. Unhealed wounds don't just go away on their own. They get worse.

Healing is not instant. It's a sacred process. Some scars fade quickly. Others require painful soul surgery. You can't microwave wholeness. Kate's physical rehab taught her how to surrender to the slowness of healing. God used her pain to slow her down—not to punish her but to form her. He wants to do the same for you. Philippians 1:6 promises, "He who started a good work in you will carry it on to completion."

So don't rush the healing process. Don't resent it either. Trust Jesus. He knows what he's doing, even when it hurts. Let the wound heal. Let grace do its slow and holy work.

R: *Redeem the Pain*

When I became a father, the absence of my own dad started to sting in a new way. I remember sitting in my office, writing letters about God's forgiveness, when I heard a whisper in my soul: *Find your father.* Immediately, I fell to my office floor and cried out, "He doesn't deserve to be found. Where was he when I needed him?" In that moment of raw honesty, I surrendered my pain to God. That was the beginning of Jesus healing my father wound.

I sensed Jesus say, *You didn't deserve me finding and forgiving you, but I did. Now do the same.* I didn't want to. But I obeyed.

I found out my father was in prison. I wrote him a letter and told him that I forgave him and that I wanted him to be part of his grandchildren's lives. His response wrecked me: "Son, thank you for forgiving me. I want to know my grandchildren. And I love you." This time, I hit the floor in tears of joy. I had never heard my dad tell me he loved me.

God has redeemed my pain. In forgiving my dad, I no longer saw him with eyes of anger but with a heart of compassion. He was one of seventeen children. He likely battled mental illness that fueled his addiction. When I forgave him, God changed me. And because I was changed, we reconciled. It wasn't easy. But it was worth it.

In forgiving my father, I became better, not bitter. God didn't waste my pain. He repurposed it. He will do the same for you.

Scars don't have to be signs of shame. They can be stories of God's grace. Your pain is not wasted. It's been redeemed.

Now it's your turn.

Prayer

Father,
You see the wounds I've carried for years.
You know the anger,
the confusion,
the tears cried in silence.

Jesus,
You took all my pain on the cross.
You forgave me freely.
You loved me when I couldn't even love myself.
I surrender my pain to you.
I give you the broken places of my heart.
And I ask you to heal me the way only you can.

Holy Spirit,
Make me a person of compassion, not revenge;
a person of grace, not resentment.
Thank you for not wasting my pain.
Thank you for rewriting my story.
I trust you even when it hurts.

In Jesus' name,
amen.

Reflection Questions

1. What scar have you been hiding that God may want to heal and use to help others?

Write a letter to God, naming the scar you've been carrying and asking him what he's inviting you to do with your healing.

2. Are you rushing past your healing when God is inviting you to rest in it?

   Carve out fifteen minutes today to be still. No noise. No phone. Just you and Jesus. Reflect on Philippians 1:6. Ask him, *Where am I limping? Where am I pretending?* Then pray, *Slow me down so I can truly heal.*

CHAPTER 12

Advocate for Yourself

Jesus gave his life for you
so he could give his life to you
so he can live his life through you.

Ever since the day Josh and Matt met in day care, they were inseparable. From elementary school until tenth grade, if you saw Josh, you saw Matt. They were brothers by choice.

But everything changed in eleventh grade. Josh focused on school. He wanted more out of life. He started studying hard, dreaming of college and launching a tech company like his hero, Steve Jobs.

Matt started skipping school and running with the wrong people who were running in the wrong direction. Josh wanted an intentional path, but his best friend wanted the wide road.

Matt told Josh, "You're not fun anymore." Josh told Matt, "Getting good grades and getting into top universities is fun."

At the beginning of his downward spiral, Matt would drink and smoke weed to have fun at parties. But his substance abuse quickly became a flimsy Band-Aid over the problems he had at home. The more he self-medicated, the deeper his depression and the worse his decision-making became.

One night Matt and his friends robbed a man. The man fought back. When he stopped fighting back, they thought they had just knocked him out. He was dead. Matt was sentenced to fifty years in prison.

While Matt sat behind bars of regret and remorse, Josh graduated from Stanford and then earned his MBA from Wharton. He launched a tech company called Zoe Technologies. Within three years he was a billionaire. He stayed focused, stayed humble, and surrounded himself with wise mentors.

After two decades, Matt was released from prison early for good behavior. He was sober. He was working hard. He wanted to make things right with the people he had hurt.

He often thought about Josh, asking himself, *What if I had stayed close to him?*

As he was scrolling social media, Matt saw a post about Josh hosting a twenty-fifth anniversary party for his company. Everyone who was anyone was invited.

Matt wanted to see his old friend. He didn't want money or pity. He just wanted to say, "I'm sorry. I know I let you down. I know I hurt you. Will you forgive me?"

He put on his old dress pants, a faded shirt, and a two-sizes-too-small suit jacket that had seen its best days about three years before. With no invitation, he went anyway.

As Matt stood at the gates of the mansion, security stopped him. They looked him up and down and laughed.

"Josh didn't invite people like you. You don't belong here."

Matt pleaded, "I'm not here to cause trouble. I'm Josh's best friend. We grew up together."

They didn't believe him.

As the security team began escorting him away, from across the courtyard, Josh saw. He shouted, "Matt!"

Josh, in a full sprint, ran to Matt and tackled him in a bear hug!

The security team, not fully recognizing what was happening, said, "Sir, he doesn't meet the dress code." So Josh did something wild. He stripped off his tuxedo jacket and said, "Matt, put this on."

Matt hesitated.

"I'm serious. Put it on."

Then Josh took Matt's two-sizes-too-small jacket and put it on.

It was a great exchange. Josh's clothes for Matt's.

Josh looked at the security guards and said, "How about now? Is he well-dressed enough to enter?"

Matt walked into the party, dressed in Josh's honor, clothed in his worth.

In this parable, you are Matt. I am Matt. We've sinned against God.

We are dressed in regrets.

We're wearing shame.

We can't get into God's Kingdom because we're not dressed in the right clothes.

But Jesus saw us.

He didn't look away from us.

He ran to us.

He took our dirty, shame-stained garments of sin and wore them to the cross.

And he took off his robe of righteousness and put it on us.

> Put on the Lord Jesus Christ, and make no provision for the flesh to gratify its desires.
>
> ROMANS 13:14

> He made the one who did not know sin to be sin for us, so that in him we might become the righteousness of God.
>
> 2 CORINTHIANS 5:21

> Since we have been made right in God's sight by the blood of Christ, he will certainly save us from God's condemnation.
>
> ROMANS 5:9, NLT

We enter the Kingdom of God because we are united to Jesus and clothed in his perfect righteousness.

Imagine standing in line to enter the party and hearing Jesus say,

> *"My friend is with me. I gave him my righteousness. He's dressed for the celebration."*

God alone clothes and dresses his people for the Kingdom of God. Only the clothes of the Lamb of God will suffice.

> Those of you who were baptized into Christ have been clothed with Christ.
>
> GALATIANS 3:27

Learning to advocate for yourself means that you find your true self in being clothed in the righteousness of Christ. When you look in the mirror, see what God the Father sees: the righteousness of Jesus.

Healing happens as we see how God has dressed us. It's your new clothes that define you—not your past.

Wrecked to Heal

It was 2009. I had been invited to a church planters' roundtable in Arkansas with a handful of young church planters. Like me, they were eager, driven, ready to soak up the ins and outs of starting a church.

But God had something else in mind. I thought I was going to learn how to build a church. But God wanted to build something in me first.

Five minutes after stepping onto that campus, I called my wife. I could barely speak through the tears. I said, "Babe, I thought I came here to learn how to plant a church. But I think God brought me here to do heart surgery." Over the next two days, two Christian psychologists didn't just counsel me—they filleted my soul open. It hurt, but it was a beautiful hurting that led to greater healing. It was like when a surgeon cuts into an infected wound to remove the poison and start the process of full healing.

There was one moment I'll never forget, a moment that changed how I see myself, how I lead, and how I minister to others. They sat me in a chair and placed another chair directly across from me. Then they asked, "If Jesus were sitting in that chair, who would God the Father say is more righteous: Jesus or you?" I knew the right answer in my head. I had preached the gospel. I had studied the Bible. I knew that the blood of Jesus makes me righteous. But this truth needed to penetrate my being. I still had some wounds that needed healing.

I thought, *How can I lead a church when I lose my wallet once a week? How can I lead when I've never been on the staff of a church, when I didn't even grow up in church? How can I preach when I'm a compulsive stutterer?* And because of the abandonment I had experienced as a child, another lie that rattled around in my head was this: *People will leave you.*

But God met me there as my heart lay bare, tears streaming, insecurities exposed. I had to take him at his word. If Scripture says that through the cross Jesus exchanged my unrighteousness for his righteousness and that I am eternally united to him, then I have the righteousness of God in Christ.

Not because I earned it.

Not because I achieved it.

But because God gifted it to me.

Pure grace.

Undeserved.

Unshakable.

If I reject that truth, I'm calling God a liar. And God does not lie. The Holy Spirit has taught me that my feelings don't define truth; God does. I am learning daily, as I keep believing the truth, that my feelings eventually catch up as I rewire my mind. Not a day goes by that I don't remind myself of this reality: *I am the righteousness of Christ.* I no longer see myself as the little boy who was abandoned and abused, mocked and neglected, who saw things no child should ever see. I choose to see myself as God sees me.

The most important spiritual discipline I practice for my soul's vitality is meditating daily on who I am in Christ. I remind myself, *I am not what was done to me. I am not what I've done. I am who God says I am.*

So are you.

You are the righteousness of God in Christ.

You can advocate for your own healing by running to the throne of grace and mercy.

Take the seat across from Jesus. Look him in the eyes. And when God the Father looks at you, know this: He sees the righteousness of his Son. And that will never change.

Prayer

Father,
Thank you for the breathtaking truth that in Christ
I am the righteousness of God.

Jesus,
Your righteousness now defines me.

Holy Spirit,
When the dark powers lie, remind me of what's true.
When fear says I'm not enough, remind me that
Jesus is my enough.
When the past tries to define me, remind me that
grace has the final word.

In Jesus' mighty name I pray,
amen.

Reflection Questions

1. How would your life change if you saw yourself as the righteousness of God in Christ?

   Each morning for sixty-six days,[1] look in the mirror and declare out loud,

   "Because of Jesus, I am the righteousness of God. I'm fully known, fully loved, and fully accepted."

   Write it down. Repeat it until your heart starts to believe it.

2. How would you explain to someone that God declares them righteous by grace and how that truth reshapes their identity, relationships, and daily life?

COUNSELORS' CORNER

Advocate for Yourself

VICKEY MACLIN (PsyD, LPA)

Harvey[2] was a fifty-four-year-old divorcé who admitted that his poor decisions were the reason his marriage had ended. He stated, "I deserve everything that has happened to me." This broken man saw no value in himself. Even though he was a Christ follower, Harvey believed that God was holding him accountable for all the wrong he had done. Not once did he speak of what had been done for him by God. Harvey wallowed in what he considered his unlovable, unredeemable state. He believed his past decisions could not be forgiven, which resulted in him dealing with depression.

Harvey believed he was beyond hope because of his past behaviors. When people believe that there is nothing good in them, it can result in feelings of insecurity and emptiness, which can lead to isolation. But hearing someone else voice truths about you is not what changes you. Change only comes when you speak words of truth about yourself *to yourself.* It was not until Harvey could acknowledge "If Scripture says that through the cross Jesus exchanged my unrighteousness for his righteousness and I am eternally united with him, then I am the righteousness of God in Christ" that his depression began to lift. Change required this beloved child of God to advocate for himself with truth that helped him see his true self.

PART 4

L: *Living* from *Love*, *Not* for *Love*

You are already loved. Live like it.

CHAPTER 13

Let Go of Striving

God: I love you! I have never not loved you.
You: But why do you love me?
God: I love you because I love you. I am love.
I created you so I could love you.

Ervin was eleven years old the first time he tasted alcohol. At a family gathering, he and his cousins stumbled upon the stash of beer and wine the adults had hidden away. His cousins took a sip, winced, and spit it out. Ervin liked it. He kept drinking until he passed out. His cousins had to carry him into the house. He spent the rest of the afternoon throwing up.

When he finally woke up, his great-grandmother sat beside him and gently said, "Son, you shouldn't drink." For a little while, he listened. But by the time Erwin started playing football in college, his great-grandmother's words faded. The craving had already taken root. What had started as an innocent sip became a death spiral. And what seemed like fun became a heavy chain.

From the very beginning, Ervin realized he could never stop at one drink.

Alcohol became his comfort when life hurt.

It became his courage when he felt small.

It became his crutch when the pressure grew.

It became his escape when he wanted to hide.

Even when he was a boy, drinking made Ervin feel whole until the effects wore off and his heart was even more frayed.

For a while, alcohol quieted the noise in his mind. It numbed the ache of growing up without a father. It helped him bury the wounds of abandonment. When Ervin was drunk, he didn't have to feel. He didn't have to face himself. The alcohol gave him false confidence. It made him bold in all the wrong ways. It fueled his ungodly pursuit of women, wine, and wealth.

Being inebriated let Ervin chase those vices without feeling guilty about it. For a time, he got what he wanted. He became a successful corporate executive. This cleared a path for him to own multiple liquor stores. He had the women. He had the money. He also had a hollow soul.

As months slipped into years, the weight of it all became too much. Nothing was enough.

Not the women.

Not the wine.

Not the wealth.

Ervin stopped going to work. He was done with life.

He loaded his truck with alcohol and found a secluded place to consume it. He spent four months trying to drink himself to death.

In his despair, Ervin cried out to God, "I'm done. Just give me death." But in the middle of his darkness, the light broke through. He heard a voice say, "I don't give death. I give life. Get up."

Ervin was gripped by God's strength. He went home, walked into the house, looked at his wife, and said, "I'm ready. I want to go to treatment."

By the time Ervin reached rehab, alcoholism had stolen everything from him.

His business.

His family.

His health.

His relationships.

And his will to live.

In rehab, Ervin saw that his addiction hadn't just wrecked his own life; it had wounded everyone who loved him. Addiction is never a solo struggle. The addict suffers, but so do the parents, the spouse, the children, and the friends. They're all pulled into the addict's chaos.

Ervin's spiritual eyes were opened too. His addiction wasn't just a habit. It was sin that had isolated him from God, opening doors to dark powers he didn't even realize he had invited in. He felt the weight of the demonic oppression that so often hides behind addiction's empty promises.

Addiction is cruel. It strips you down. It destroys who you are. And then it covers you in shame and self-hatred.

But in the rubble of his life, Ervin found what he never expected: the grace of God through the Word of God and the treatment center staff. Hope began to replace despair.

Ervin spent thirty-one hard, healing days in rehab. The staff welcomed him—not with shallow comfort but with firm, compassionate discipline. They loved him enough to tell him the truth. They helped him unpack years of buried pain. And most importantly, they led Ervin into the loving, merciful arms of Jesus. Jesus is the only One who could forgive Ervin's sin and empower him to break free from the chains of alcoholism.

In that sacred space called rehab, Ervin was forced to confront the monster he had become. But even more, he came face-to-face with the God who tames monsters. The God who takes addicts, liars, and wanderers and says, *You are my beloved.*

Ervin began to understand that he didn't have to earn God's love. In rehab, Ervin experienced gospel-centered recovery. He surrounded himself with gracious, Jesus-loving people who held him accountable and taught him coping skills. He learned to walk in God's love and the Holy Spirit's power. That rhythm of grace keeps him sober to this day.

Ervin is a wounded healer. He leads a recovery ministry to help others find the same hope and healing he's experienced. He and his team walk with people out of addiction and into freedom through faith-based treatment.

The powers of darkness thought that they had captured another poor soul. But Jesus wrote a new story.

Living *from* Love, Not *for* Love

Ervin's healing began with one eternal, life-changing truth: God is love. Love isn't just something God *does*; love is who God *is*. It was the relentless, redeeming love of God, revealed through Jesus, that washed away Ervin's guilt and evicted his shame. For years, self-hatred had kept him in chains. That's what addiction does. It feeds on your brokenness and convinces you that you're beyond repair.

The love of Christ taught Ervin to see himself as God sees him. He began to love himself because he is loved by the One who knows him fully and still calls him beloved. It wasn't willpower that healed Ervin. It was love. *Real* love. Life-giving, soul-restoring love. And that same love is available to you. As the apostle Paul, the author of Ephesians, put it:

> I pray . . . that Christ may dwell in your hearts through faith. I pray that you, being rooted and firmly established in love, may be able to comprehend with all the saints what is the length and width, height and depth of God's love, and to know Christ's love that surpasses knowledge, so that you may be filled with all the fullness of God.
>
> Now to him who is able to do above and beyond all that we ask or think according to the power that works in us—to him be glory in the church and in Christ Jesus to all generations, forever and ever. Amen.
>
> **EPHESIANS 3:16-21**

LOVE

Jose and Marie married right after college. They met at a party their sophomore year, full of hope and dreams, like so many young couples. But neither of them realized that when they said "I do," they were also saying "I do" to the invisible backpacks they carried, weighed down with family dysfunction, unhealed wounds, and insecurities passed down from their parents.

Marie, who had been raised by harsh and critical parents, carried that same spirit into their home, and Jose became the target of her pain. He wanted to seek marriage counseling, but she refused. "That's for weak people," she told him. "If my parents stayed married forty years without counseling, so can we."

Jose felt small. Disrespected. Unseen. But he kept trying. He wanted to honor his vows before God and before Marie. She even gave him a list of things he needed to do to satisfy her, but no matter how hard Jose tried, he could never get it right.

Then Marie got sick. Cancer came fast. And after twenty-five years of marriage, Jose found himself a widower, grieving a wife he had loved—and a marriage that had been complicated, painful, and filled with unspoken sorrow.

Jose wasn't looking for a new relationship. His focus was on raising the kids and being the best father he could be. But one evening, some friends from church invited him over for dinner and introduced him to a widow named Ann. Jose and Ann connected first as friends. And in time, their friendship bloomed into love.

Jose and Ann were married and built a beautiful blended family together. Life felt lighter. Kinder. Safe.

But then one afternoon, while cleaning the garage, Jose opened an old box. Right on top was the list Marie had made all those years ago. For a moment, fear shot through his chest—old memories, old accusations, old shame. But as he kept reading, something unexpected happened. Tears of joy filled his eyes.

He realized he was doing every single thing on that list and more, not out of fear, not to prove himself, but because Ann loved him.

Ann respected him.

Ann championed him.

Ann believed in him.

Ann loved him.

Ann was proud of him.

Jose wasn't living to earn Ann's love. He was living *from* Ann's love.

That's the difference between performance-based religion and grace-based life in Christ. Performance says, "Obey God so he will love you." But grace says, "Because you are loved by God, you obey."

Performance-based living keeps score and tells you, "You didn't score high enough."

Grace-based living tells you, "Jesus is your score. And he's your enough."

Love brings the best out of you.

To help you remember how to live *from* God's love, not *for* it, learn to LOVE:

L: *Let Go of Your Résumé*

You will experience the love of God when you stop thinking and acting like you must earn it.

God doesn't love you because you handed him your résumé filled with all your accomplishments. God's love is rooted in his eternal, unchanging character. God is love. And his love is manifest in Jesus and his sacrifice for you. Let go of striving and just receive it.

> Love consists in this: not that we loved God, but that he loved us and sent his Son to be the atoning sacrifice for our sins.
>
> **1 JOHN 4:10**

O: *Open Your Heart to Grace*

Like me, you've probably done things you'd like no one to ever know.

Shame and guilt make us believe we're unworthy of love. But grace says otherwise. When you open your heart to grace, you stop running from God and start relying on his loyal love.

> You are saved by grace through faith, and this is not from yourselves; it is God's gift—not from works, so that no one can boast.
>
> **EPHESIANS 2:8-9**

V: *Value Your Identity in Christ*

From an early age, we are taught to build our worth on how good we are at life. This unstable foundation turns us into our own gods. This keeps us from God. Who needs God when you think you are god?

When you live from God's love, you begin to see your worth because of the price God paid for you. That's love.

> You know that you were redeemed from your empty way of life inherited from your ancestors, not with perishable things like silver or gold, but with the precious blood of Christ, like that of an unblemished and spotless lamb.
>
> **1 PETER 1:18-19**

E: *Experience God's Presence Daily*

Jesus is not a means to an end. He is the end. He simply wants to love you.

The God of love resides in you. He wants you to spend time with him in everything you do.

He loves to love you.

Set your mind on him.

Keep your eyes on the cross.

Behold him and let him take hold of you.

> He predestined us to be adopted as sons through Jesus Christ for himself, according to the good pleasure of his will, to the praise of his glorious grace that he lavished on us in the Beloved One.
>
> **EPHESIANS 1:5-6**

Prayer

Father, Son, and Holy Spirit,
Your love pursued me when I was lost in shame.
Your mercy met me in the dark and called me into the light.
I confess that self-hatred has kept me bound for too long.
But today I choose to believe what you say about me.
Through Jesus, you have washed away my guilt
and broken my chains.
Teach me to live *from* your love, not *for* it.
Help me see myself through the eyes of grace.
Let your love heal me, reshape me,
and empower me to love others well.
In Jesus' name,
amen.

Reflection Questions

1. How would your life be different if you believed that God loves you in Christ by grace and not by you earning it? Are you still trying to earn the love that's already been given to you?

   Write down your answer.

2. Have you opened your heart to grace? Or are shame and guilt still running the show? If you were in a court of law, what would the evidence of your life demonstrate: grace-based living or performance-based living?

   Spend ten minutes reading Ephesians 3:16-21 slowly.

   Ask God to help you feel the depth of his love.

   Write a letter to yourself from God's perspective. What would your heavenly Father say to the wounded parts of you? Let his words silence the shame.

CHAPTER 14

Lean into Lessons, Not Losses

God turns our losses into lessons.

One man was a respected pastor. His sermons were soaked in grace, and he wrote soul-stirring hymns. Echoes of Christ rang through every word he spoke.

He wasn't only concerned with getting people to heaven. He cared about justice on earth, especially justice for people of African descent who were enslaved. His ministry was so impactful that a young politician he discipled, a man named William, went on to help abolish the evil of slavery—not only in Britain but eventually in America through his influence as well.

William's mentor was once the captain of a slave ship. He chose to become a human trafficker because it was easy money. The conditions on his ship, and many others like it, were horrific. Shackled men, women, and children lay beneath the deck in their own vomit, feces, and blood. Many died. Their bodies were tossed into the ocean, lost in the horror of the Middle Passage.

The man who preached the gospel and advocated for the end of slavery was the same man who had captained a slave ship. His name is John Newton, and his story is a testimony to God's grace.

One night, caught in a violent storm at sea, John cried out to God in desperation. God saved him not only from the storm surrounding him but also from the storm within. The grace of Jesus transformed a man who had once enslaved others into a man who would spend the rest of his life proclaiming the freedom found in Christ, both spiritually and physically.[1]

Instead of letting his failures define him, John Newton chose to let God redefine him.

He let grace reengineer his story. And so can you.

He chose to let God turn his guilt into purpose, his scars into songs, his shame into a testimony. The same man who once enslaved others penned the words "Amazing grace—how sweet the sound—that saved a wretch like me!"[2]

After eighty-two years of life, John's memory was just about gone. When reflecting on what he remembered of his life, he said: "that I am a great sinner—and that Christ is a great Savior!"[3]

His tombstone reads, "John Newton, once an infidel and libertine, a servant of slaves in Africa, was, by the rich mercy of our Lord and Savior Jesus Christ, preserved, restored, pardoned, and appointed to preach the faith he had long labored to destroy!"[4]

Grace > Regret

Psychologist Dr. Melanie Greenberg describes regret as "a negative cognitive or emotional state that involves blaming ourselves for a bad outcome, feeling a sense of loss or sorrow at what might have been, or wishing we could undo a previous choice that we made."[5]

Regret doesn't just stay in our minds. It drips poison into our souls. When we let regret grow, it becomes a weed that chokes us. The past replays in our minds like a broken record, stuck in self-blame and disgrace. Regret makes us relive what we did years ago and the poor choice we made yesterday. We replay it over and over, wishing we could go back and choose better, choose wiser. But we can't. And even when we know in our minds that God has forgiven us, regret still eats away at our hearts.

Regret is cruel. It steals our hope. It keeps us from reengaging with life. And when left unresolved, regret can lead to depression and other mental health struggles.[6]

But God's grace is greater than regret. Grace shuts the mouth of regret. Grace speaks life over us: *You are not the sum of your worst decisions.*

Your past sins have been nailed to the cross. Jesus' righteousness has been nailed to you.

Friend, your past is a place to learn from, not a place to live in.

It may have shaped you, but it doesn't have to shackle you.

Don't build a home in the ruins of regret. God's grace invites you into a new neighborhood, one he's built with his own hands.

LESSON

Like John Newton discovered, every scar can carry wisdom. Every loss can become a lesson. And hands that once oppressed can become hands that liberate.

If we choose to lean into the LESSON, we'll discover how to live from what life has taught us, not from what life has taken from us. Take the steps today to grow stronger, not stay stuck.

L: *Look Back with Honesty*

God's grace gives us the emotional strength to face our pasts without fear. It's only when we look at our sins honestly—the pain we've caused, the people we've hurt—that we begin to grasp the depth of God's mercy. We don't heal by sugarcoating our past behavior. When we stop hiding and start acknowledging our regrets, we give God something real to redeem.

E: *Embrace God's Grace*

Embracing God's grace is harder than it sounds because grace confronts our pride. We want to stand on our own two feet. We want to prove our worth. We want to carry our own burdens. Asking for help feels weak. And letting someone else pay for what we've done feels unfair. But that's the gospel. It's only for those who are too weak to save themselves—which is all of us. When our failure collides with the faithfulness of Jesus, we are reborn.

Your story isn't over because of your past sin. God's grace is bigger than your regret.

S: *See the Story God Is Writing*

When an author writes a book, the editor uses a red pen to mark what needs to change so the story can be stronger. In your life, God didn't use red ink; he used the red blood of Jesus. His sacrifice has rewritten your story. His paintbrush (the cross) has redeemed you.

S: *Speak Life Over Yourself*

Regret can crash over us like a series of relentless waves, trying to pull us into a sea of despair. It overwhelms us with lies like

> *You'll never change.*

and

> *You've ruined too much.*

But God will not let us drown!

When the waves rise, we fight back by speaking the words of Christ over our lives.

His words anchor us. God calls you

- *forgiven*:[7] Your sins are not your identity. God's grace is.
- *holy*:[8] You are set apart as God's child—not because you're perfect but because he is.
- *blameless*:[9] You are covered by the blood of Jesus. No accusation can stick.
- *chosen*:[10] You have been handpicked by God for a purpose that cannot be taken from you.
- *beloved*:[11] You are delighted in, cherished, pursued.

- *a new creation*:[12] The old is gone. You live in a new reality pulsating with the life of Christ.

Regret has no power over you, because grace is greater.

O: *Own Your Growth*

The people who grow beyond regret and self-loathing are the ones who take ownership of their past behavior. They don't blame others. They own their own behavior. And by God's grace, they grow from the experience.

People who stay stuck in regret often get trapped in blame. As psychologist Arash Emamzadeh explains, "Blaming *others* appears to *reduce* a person's *own negative emotions* (e.g., anger, guilt, shame). This may explain why poor emotion regulators prefer to point fingers at others rather than hold themselves responsible."[13]

But blame doesn't heal. It delays growth. Real healing begins when we stop avoiding and start owning. Growth happens when we say, "That was me. I did that."

You can't change the past, but you *can* let God change you.

N: *Never Waste the Pain*

I was raised to survive. My background made me tough. If I didn't look out for me, who would? This led to a life of self-preservation and sin.

For years, regret chased me, guilted me, shamed me. When I ran out of places to run, Jesus was waiting for me to give him my regret. He's repurposed it. He expanded my shrunken, fearful, selfish heart to that of a big-hearted pastor who loves people.

I don't know what your regret is. But God can take the wreckage of your past and turn it into a testimony of redemption.

With God, nothing is wasted.

In his loving-kindness, there are no losses—only lessons that lead to healing and hope.

Prayer

Father,
When I look at the wreckage of my past,
I often feel regret.
But you see raw materials for redemption.
Thank you for loving me when I didn't love myself.

Jesus,
I give you my regrets.
I lay down blaming and self-loathing.
I choose your healing.

Holy Spirit,
Help me take ownership of my healing.
Give me courage to face the truth and to receive grace.
Write a new story in my life.
Turn my losses into lessons.

In Jesus' name,
amen.

Reflection Questions

1. What are some of your regrets? How would your life be different if you stopped living in the ruins of your past?

   Create two columns on a sheet of paper. On one side, write down some of your regrets. On the other, write what is true of you in Christ: You are forgiven, chosen, loved, new.

2. What lesson is God teaching you from your past regrets?

   Reflect on who might be encouraged by some of the lessons you've learned. Share them with that person.

COUNSELORS' CORNER

Deal With It

JIM CRESS (MA, LPC, CSAT, CMAT)

In his classic song "My Way," Frank Sinatra proclaims, "Regrets, I've had a few."[14] You may be thinking (as I do), *I've had more than a few regrets in my life!* Losses and regrets can become powerful teachers of insight and wisdom if we allow them to. When I invite those I counsel to look at some of the painful failures of their pasts, I encourage them, "Deal with your past; don't dwell in your past. Walk through your past; don't wallow in your past." God is always ready and wanting to redeem our losses. In fact, God has a master plan to use your regrets to help others find true freedom in Christ and see their life stories redeemed for his Kingdom purposes. Instead of becoming bitter over regrets or living with a victim mentality, sit with your losses. It is often helpful to work with a trusted Christian counselor, who can act as a safe, wise guide as you explore your past. You see, people don't merely have stories; we *are* stories! In fact, our life stories are far more epic and awesome than those of any bestselling novel or movie. Ask God for insight, understanding, and wisdom to see your regrets as sages guiding you along the pathway of your ongoing character transformation in Jesus Christ!

CHAPTER 15

Let God Forgive Through You

Those who were able to forgive their former enemies were able also to return to the outside world and rebuild their lives, no matter what the physical scars. Those who nursed their bitterness remained invalids. It was as simple and as horrible as that.

CORRIE TEN BOOM

He sat alone in a dark room, and the tears began to fall—slowly at first, then pouring like they'd been waiting years to escape. They weren't tears of despair. They were tears of forgiveness.

After a lifetime of forgiving others for the wounds they'd caused, he had finally reached the last person left to forgive—himself. Forgiving others had always felt easier. But forgiving himself felt impossible. Somewhere along the way, he had swallowed the lie that God could forgive everyone else's sins but his were somehow different . . . heavier . . . unforgivable. He held himself to a higher standard than anyone else. He beat himself up with thoughts like *I should have known better* and *I should have been stronger*. His own self-righteousness and unrealistic expectations had become a prison.

With blurry eyes, he fumbled through his Bible, desperate for a word from God. His tears made the page hard to read, but his fingers landed on Romans 8:1:

> Therefore, there is now no condemnation for those in Christ Jesus.

In that moment, the Holy Spirit whispered to his heart:

Son, you are in Christ. He took your condemnation.
You are fully forgiven. Your sins are eternally forgotten.
Every charge against you has been dropped.
Your guilt has been erased.
Who Christ is now defines who you are.

And just like that—like someone flipping on a light switch—he began to forgive himself.

He became less anxious.

He became less judgmental.

He became more merciful.

That man in the dark room was me—sitting in the shadows until the light of God's forgiveness broke through and set me free.

Save Your Own Life

When we forgive the people who have hurt us, including ourselves, we may be literally saving our own lives.

Living in unforgiveness is like inhaling carbon monoxide.

It's slowly killing you from the inside out. Unforgiveness wrecks our bodies, minds, and relationships. Holding on to resentment doesn't hurt the other person. It keeps us hurt.

Every time you replay what they did to you, you're allowing them to injure you all over again. Living in unforgiveness is like taking the very knife they used to stab you and turning it on yourself.

Forgiveness is how you stop bleeding.

When you forgive, you're not validating what they did. You're taking a stand: *I won't let what you did destroy me anymore.*

Forgiveness is not weakness. It's power.

When you forgive, you reflect the heart of God, who forgave you.

When you forgive, you reclaim your life.

When you forgive, you break the cycle of revenge.

When Jesus commands us to forgive, it's not to burden us. It's to set us free.

> "Pray like this: . . .
>
> Forgive us our sins,
> as we have forgiven those who sin against us."
>
> **JESUS (MATTHEW 6:12, NLT)**

The Hidden War

Even science affirms that the cost of unforgiveness is too high. Unforgiveness hijacks your nervous system and devastates your mental, emotional, and physical health.[1] When you ruminate on what someone did to wound you, your brain reactivates that pain as if it's happening all over again. That triggers your fight-or-flight response. Your body floods with cortisol, a stress hormone. This leads to chronic anxiety, poor sleeping habits, and emotional burnout.

Constantly replaying something that wounded you is like picking at a scab over and over. The wound never gets a chance to heal. Instead of moving forward, you stay stuck in the pain. Ruminating on how someone hurt you will only make you spiral deeper into sadness, bitterness, and eventually depression.

Unforgiveness doesn't just weigh on your heart. It wears down your brain. It breaks down your body. The constant stress can damage your hippocampus, the part of your brain that helps you remember, learn, and stay emotionally balanced.[2] And research shows that unforgiveness is connected to

- high blood pressure;
- a weakened immune system;
- heart disease;
- chronic pain; and
- increased inflammation, which is a root cause of many diseases.[3]

Forgiveness is medicine. And sometimes medicine tastes awful, but the results are for your good.

Science agrees with what Scripture has always said: Forgiveness is holistically good for you. A study of more than fourteen hundred Americans found that those who practiced forgiveness experienced better physical and mental health than those who didn't. Another study revealed that people with high levels of forgiveness had lower levels of stress and fewer mental health symptoms across their lives than those with lower levels.[4]

Forgiveness is oxygen for the heart. It doesn't mean forgetting the hell that someone unleashed on you or that you unleashed on yourself. It means releasing it so healing can begin. When we choose to forgive, we choose to move toward emotional and mental restoration. Forgiveness shifts us out of merely surviving and into thriving.

The Relational Cost

Unforgiveness is like a spiritual plague. It clogs the spiritual arteries of your heart and keeps love from flowing freely. When past hurts go unhealed and unforgiven, they become barriers to intimacy and trust with God, yourself, and others. Just like plaque buildup can block the heart and cause a heart attack, bitterness and resentment block us from truly letting people or God in.

Unforgiveness tells us, *Protect yourself. Don't get too close. They'll hurt you like the others did.*

So we pull away. We build emotional walls. And in trying to protect ourselves from pain, we also block ourselves from love.

Early in my marriage, I found myself pulling away from emotional intimacy with my wife—not because she'd hurt me but because others had. I hadn't forgiven the people who had betrayed me when I was younger, so I projected that hurt onto her. I kept waiting for rejection that never came. And in doing so, I missed out on the fullness of her love.

Unforgiveness distorts your vision. It becomes the lens through which you see everyone. And it even creates distance between you and God. The heart that can't let other people in struggles to let God in too.

Forgiveness is the key that opens the door to healing and relational intimacy. It's time for you to discover life on the other side.

What You Need to Know About Forgiveness

Years ago, in a men's small group, someone asked me, "How did you forgive your father after he left you?" I sat in silence for a moment, letting the weight of the question settle. Then I said, "How could I not forgive my dad when my heavenly Father has forgiven me? How could I hold back forgiveness when God has forgiven me of so much?"

Here's the deal: Forgiven people forgive people. Jesus said, "If you forgive others their offenses, your heavenly Father will forgive you as well."[5] When you've tasted the sweet forgiveness of God, you discover that you can forgive people who have left a bitter taste in your soul.

That's not to say it's natural or even easy to do so. You will need to rely on the power of the Holy Spirit to forgive. God will provide the needed power. Do you have the will to forgive?

Remember:

- *Forgiveness takes patience.* If you're struggling to forgive, don't beat yourself up. Forgiving people who have hurt you takes time, and we often do it over and over again with the help of the Holy Spirit. It takes time for Jesus to tenderize your heart with his forgiveness. The more his mercy soaks into your soul, the more you'll find yourself wanting to extend forgiveness to others.
- *Forgiveness requires dependence.* We can't forgive ourselves in our own strength. But the same Spirit who

raised Jesus from the dead lives in you. He can give you the power to do what feels impossible. Ask him. God loves to help his children experience freedom.

- *Forgiveness is a lifelong journey.* God forgives instantly and completely. But for us, forgiveness is something we often must practice multiple times per day. That's what Jesus meant when he said to forgive "seventy times seven."[6] Every time the pain resurfaces, we forgive again—not to excuse the offense but to keep our hearts from paying the high price of unforgiveness.
- *Forgiveness and justice can walk together.* If someone sinned against you and broke the law, choosing to forgive them can happen alongside contacting the proper authorities. Seeking justice isn't revenge. It's part of healing and protection for you and for others.
- *Forgiveness doesn't mean staying in an abusive relationship.* You can forgive someone and still set healthy boundaries with them. Jesus never called you to be a punching bag, physically or emotionally. You can love and forgive someone from a distance.

Forgiveness is the path to peace. Forgiveness is not easy. But we do it in God's strength.

How to Forgive What's Hard to Forget

Before my grandmother passed, she shared something with me she had carried since she was a little girl. Someone who was supposed to love and protect her had hurt her deeply instead. The trauma cut so far into her soul that for decades she imagined ways she would make him pay for what he had done to her and to others. I could see the pain and anger etched into her face as she shared about her experience.

For fifty years, that wound had fed on my grandmother's heart. The memories had kept reopening the hurt, and she was exhausted from reliving the same pain again and again. She didn't want to be rewounded by the past anymore. With God's help, she chose the brave road of forgiveness. It wasn't instant. It took prayer. It took tears. It took intentional, deep internal work. But little by little, the grip of that trauma loosened, and the God who heals met her in the place where she had been carrying her pain alone for far too long.

Forgiveness doesn't just happen. It's something we choose. Choosing forgiveness takes courage. The Holy Spirit will supply the courage you need. And he doesn't run out of strength, so you will be continually empowered to forgive.

Dr. Everett Worthington, a renowned clinical psychologist and forgiveness expert, has developed a five-step forgiveness program called REACH:[7]

R: Recall the hurt.
E: Empathize with the offender.
A: Altruistically forgive.
C: Commit to forgiveness.
H: Hold on to forgiveness.

This process of healing is not just psychology. It's biblical. It echoes the way Christ forgives us and calls us to forgive others.

R: *Recall the Hurt*

I tried to bury what had happened to me when I was eleven years old. I pushed it down. But the pain didn't go away; it just hid in the shadows, shaping how I saw the world and how I saw myself. Eventually, I had to face it. I had to name it for what it was: abuse.

As a teenager, I told some friends the story of what had happened. They laughed and said it sounded cool. It wasn't. Over the years, I minimized it. But in my mid-forties, I knew I needed to forgive the person who had scarred me. Not because they deserved it but because I needed to be free. And Jesus commands me to forgive.

Jesus never asks us to ignore our wounds or pretend they didn't happen. Look at his scars. They're proof that sin is real. And the resurrection is proof that healing is real too.

Forgiveness begins when we stop denying the wound. Jesus commands our souls to be brave enough to name the hurt.[8]

We remember it. We name it. We feel it. But we don't stay there.

E: *Empathize with the Offender*

Empathy is the holy ability to feel what someone else feels, to step into their story, even if their story has brought pain into yours. When it came time to forgive the person who had wounded me, I knew I couldn't do it with my own strength. So God gave me something unexpected: empathy. He opened my eyes to see that this person wasn't just a perpetrator of pain; they were also a victim of it.

They had suffered abuse. They battled undiagnosed mental illness. They were shackled by addiction. Their life was a storm of unhealed wounds. I'm not excusing what they did. What they did was wrong. But I am choosing to see them the way Jesus sees them: as a broken person in desperate need of healing love.

Empathy is the work of the Holy Spirit. He changes the lens through which we see others. He helps us stop looking at people through the eyes of bitterness and start seeing them through the eyes of Jesus. Remember how Jesus, bloodied and crucified, looked down at the very people who tortured him and prayed, "Father, forgive them; for they know not what they do."[9] That wasn't weakness. That was divine power. That was God's love in action.

When we understand the pain that shaped the people who have hurt us, our hearts change. Compassion begins to sprout where anger once grew.

Forgiveness starts to flow where resentment used to rule.

Empathy doesn't erase the wound. But it becomes the soil where mercy can grow. Empathizing with those who have betrayed us is not natural. It's supernatural. It's a path the Holy Spirit will walk with you, one courageous step at a time.

A: *Altruistically Forgive*

Altruistic forgiveness means forgiving without expecting anything in return. In forgiveness, we don't just release the offender. We also release ourselves. That's the reward of forgiveness: your own freedom.

Freedom to heal.

Freedom to love.

Freedom to live again.

Freedom to free others who are lost in unforgiveness.

An eye for an eye keeps us all from seeing properly. Forgiveness opens our eyes to see.

We didn't earn the forgiveness of Jesus. He died for us while we were sinners. So in return, by his power, we can become "kind and compassionate to one another, forgiving one another, just as God also forgave you in Christ."[10]

C: *Commit to Forgiveness*

I had to learn that forgiveness is not a feeling. It's a decision rooted in obeying Jesus. Feelings come and go, but we choose forgiveness because Christ chose to forgive us. This is a daily commitment to walk in the Holy Spirit's power.

The dark powers will attack us with words like *Remember what they did? Make them pay!*

But we stand firm and declare, "I will forgive because Christ has forgiven me."

H: *Hold on to Forgiveness*

Forgiveness is a road that we will travel for the rest of our lives. It's a blessed journey of carrying the cross.

Life is much better when we hold on to the cross instead of holding on to unforgiveness. Forgiveness is a refusal to let bitterness take hold of you.

A life marked by forgiveness means praying for those who have hurt us and trusting that God is the ultimate Healer and Judge.

Please REACH for healing. The freedom you long for is on the other side of "I forgive you."

But I tell you, love your enemies and pray for those who persecute you.

JESUS, THE SON OF GOD (MATTHEW 5:44)

Prayer

Father,
I choose to forgive not because they deserve it
but because you forgave me.
Not because I feel like it, but because I want to be free.

Jesus,
Thank you for forgiving me when I didn't deserve it.
While I was still caught in my sin,
you stretched out your arms in love and died for me.
I want to forgive like you forgive.
But I confess, it's hard.
The pain is real. The wounds go deep.

Holy Spirit,
Grow empathy in my heart.
Help me see those who have hurt me not just as offenders
but as broken people in need of your healing too.
Make me more like you.
Kind. Compassionate. Forgiving.
Because I've been forgiven.

In Jesus' name,
amen.

Reflection Questions

1. What is a part of your story in which you struggle with forgiveness? How would your life be different if you practiced REACH?

   REACH for healing. Practice Dr. Worthington's five-step path:

   R: Recall the hurt without minimizing it.
   E: Empathize with the other person's brokenness, even if you never excuse their actions.
   A: Altruistically forgive by choosing freedom, not revenge.
   C: Commit to forgiveness—write it down, speak it out, make it real.
   H: Hold on to forgiveness—because bitterness will try to take it back.

   Tell someone safe. Share your story with a counselor, pastor, or trusted friend who can walk with you through this process. You don't have to heal alone.

2. Which of the five steps in Dr. Worthington's path to forgiveness is hardest for you?

COUNSELORS' CORNER

Let God Forgive Through You

VICKEY MACLIN (PsyD, LPA)

Growing up, people learn ways to think about themselves based on events that happen. The experience of events results in developing schemas, enduring mental structures that affect cognitive processing about oneself.[11] Schemas become filters of how people predict what will happen in their lives.

Joan,[12] a forty-three-year-old woman, was molested from age six to twelve. The schema she developed centered around the resulting sexual trauma. She had a temperament based on that traumatization and resulting cognitive beliefs about herself. Much like Derwin Gray's grandmother, who carried wounds from her past for half a century, this young woman was deeply affected by her trauma decades later. Joan experienced men as only being interested in her to obtain sexual gratification. Her experience also resulted in her seeing herself as only being able to have relationships for the same purpose.

By the time Joan came to counseling, she was disgusted with herself and with men. She had learned to use men but had grown to hate herself. The way she got through each day was to self-medicate with drugs and alcohol.

In counseling Joan admitted that she wanted to change. It took months, but change happened as she began to REACH. The first step—*recall the hurt*—was the most difficult. She had to own her emotions and also not blame herself for others' behavior. The journey was only possible because she had reached out. She demonstrated that change is possible when one begins the journey toward healing. After two years of counseling, Joan became a different person, one who continued to use skills she had learned to keep experiencing further healing.

CHAPTER 16

Become a Wounded Healer

Beloved wounded healer,

Thank you for reading It's Time to Heal: Four God-Given Steps to Restore What Life Has Shattered. *Walking with you on this long, winding, sometimes uphill road toward healing has been one of the greatest honors of my life.*

I may not know your exact story. What you've lost. What's been done to you. What you carry in the quiet places of your heart. But I know you've cried rivers of tears. I know you've tried and tried to fix your life. And I know you're tired of trying. But now you've surrendered to the One who says, "Come to me, all of you who are weary and burdened, and I will give you rest."[1]

The powers of darkness had a plan to destroy you. They wanted your trauma to be contagious, to infect your future, your children, your relationships. They hoped the pain would echo forward like a curse through future generations.

But God has a greater plan.

He took what was meant to break you and is using it to remake you.

Out of the ashes, you are rising in the power of the One who rose out of the tomb. You are holding the scarred, bloodstained hands of the risen King. You are an overcomer.

Jesus, the Resurrected One, is also the Suffering Servant. He didn't run from your pain. He ran to the cross with joy, knowing you were worth the cost. He has not only forgiven you; he's made you a child of the Father and the home of the Holy Spirit.

You are more powerful than you realize. The same power that raised Jesus from the dead now lives in you. And with that power, your scars are becoming stories of redemption. You are more than a survivor. You are more than a conqueror. You are fiercely and eternally loved.

You are not what happened to you.

You are not what you've done.

You are a blood-bought, Spirit-filled child of the Most High God with hope in your heart.

You are learning to set your mind on what is true, honorable, just, pure, lovely, and commendable. God is rewiring your brain. And that's not just neuroscience; that's discipleship. That's healing.

As the Holy Spirit helps you remember God's faithfulness, your brain begins to trust.[2]

Hope takes root.

Your heart becomes rooted like an oak tree near a river.

You begin to see your pain being transformed into purpose and losses into lessons.

Fear and anxiety don't have the last word. The peace of Christ does. You are learning to "remember the deeds of the LORD; yes, I will remember your miracles of long ago. I will consider all your works and meditate on all your mighty deeds."[3]

You're now a member of the wounded healers' club. You walked through fire. And by God's grace, you came out refined, not ruined. You carry stories that bleed with beauty.

Now take what God has done in you and tell others about his healing power. Let them know that their scars can become stories that heal.

Healing with you,
Pastor Derwin

Prayer

Father,
Thank you for walking with me through the pain,
through the heartbreak,
and through the valley I thought I wouldn't survive.
Thank you that what was meant to break me
you are using to remake me.

Jesus,
I praise you for holding my hand when
I was too tired to keep trying;
for whispering,
Come to me and I will give you rest
when the weight of life felt too heavy.
You saw every tear I cried.
You never turned away.
And now you are healing what I thought
could never be healed.
You are turning my scars into stories of grace.
You're using the ashes of my past to plant seeds of purpose.

Holy Spirit,
Help me keep remembering your faithfulness.
Let your Spirit renew my mind as I set my thoughts
on what is true, pure, and lovely.
Rewire my thinking with the truth of Scripture.
Help me live like someone who carries resurrection power.
Today I choose to trust you again.

I choose to believe that my pain is not wasted.
I choose to let my life be a testimony that says,
"God heals. God restores. God is faithful."
Let my healing bring hope to others.
Make me a wounded healer who walks with others
the way you've walked with me.

In Jesus' name,
amen.

Reflection Questions

1. Healing is contagious when wounded healers choose to let their scars become testimonies. Who are five people you know who God may want to invite into healing?

   Write down their names.

   Pray for them.

   Then ask them to read *It's Time to Heal* with you as a small group.

2. God's faithfulness on our journey shows up in the longer story he's writing. Set a reminder to reread *It's Time to Heal* a year from now!

   Write down how you have healed.

   Write the names of people you've helped heal.

Acknowledgments

It's Time to Heal is not something I wrote alone. It is the fruit of love, patience, and faith poured into my life by the people closest to me.

First, to my beautiful and courageous wife and ministry partner, Vicki. You have walked with me through wounds, questions, prayers, and hope. Your strength, wisdom, and grace steady me more than you know. I am better because I do life and ministry with you.

Second, to my children, Presley and Jeremiah. You have taught me far more about love, resilience, and joy than I could ever teach you. Watching you grow into adults has shaped my heart and reminded me why healing matters.

Third, to the Transformation Church family. Your love for Jesus, your hunger for wholeness, and your willingness to walk toward healing together have deeply encouraged me. This book carries your stories, your prayers, and your faith.

Fourth, to my agent, Alexander Field. Thank you for believing in me as a writer and for championing this message with conviction and clarity.

Finally, to NavPress and my editor, the wise and gifted Caitlyn Carlson. Your care, insight, and editorial excellence have strengthened both this book and my voice as a writer. I am deeply grateful for our gospel partnership.

This book exists because of you. Thank you for walking with me on the journey toward healing.

Counselors' Corner Experts

Jim Cress (MA, LPC, CSAT, CMAT) is a licensed professional counselor, a licensed clinical mental health counselor, and a life coach, specializing in sex addiction, marital counseling, and trauma. Jim is a group leader for Onsite Workshops (near Nashville, Tennessee) and a national conference speaker with the American Association of Christian Counselors. He is also one of the cohosts of the *Therapy & Theology* podcast with Lysa TerKeurst. Jim and his wife, Jessica, live in Charlotte, North Carolina, and have three children and five grandchildren.

Vickey Maclin (PsyD, LPA) teaches at Gordon-Conwell Theological Seminary, where she also serves as the associate director of graduate programs in counseling. She is a licensed psychological associate in North Carolina. She received her master's in counseling from Reformed Theological Seminary and her PsyD in clinical psychology from Wheaton College.

Notes

CHAPTER 0 | WOULD YOU LIKE TO GET WELL?

1. Romans 8:37.
2. Romans 5:1.
3. Philippians 2:12-13.
4. 1 Peter 1:5.
5. Galatians 4:19.
6. Ephesians 4:24, NLT.
7. Colossians 1:28.
8. John 5:6, NLT.

CHAPTER 1 | HIDE NO MORE

1. Psalm 56:8.
2. "The Twelve Steps," Alcoholics Anonymous, accessed December 10, 2025, https://www.aa.org/the-twelve-steps.
3. Matthew 5:3.
4. Genesis 50:20; also see Romans 8:28.
5. Genesis 37, 39–50.
6. Genesis 45:5.

CHAPTER 2 | HEAD HOME

1. Luke 15:11-32.
2. See Hebrews 8:12.
3. 2 Corinthians 5:21.
4. Galatians 4:6-7.

5. Ephesians 1:13-14.
6. Romans 8:1.

CHAPTER 3 | HEAL YOUR HEART

1. John 4:10.
2. 2 Corinthians 5:17.
3. Proverbs 4:23.
4. Ephesians 3:16-17.
5. "10 Ridiculously Simple Ways to Boost Your Brain," Amen Clinics, February 1, 2022, https://www.amenclinics.com/blog/10-ridiculously-simple-ways-to-boost-your-brain.
6. "Brainwork: The Power of Neuroplasticity," Cleveland Clinic, December 13, 2023, https://health.clevelandclinic.org/neuroplasticity.
7. Romans 12:2.
8. "What Is Cognitive Behavioral Therapy?," American Psychological Association, 2017, https://www.apa.org/ptsd-guideline/patients-and-families/cognitive-behavioral.
9. Name was changed to protect her privacy.
10. Gabor Maté with Daniel Maté, *The Myth of Normal: Trauma, Illness, and Healing in a Toxic Culture* (Avery, 2022), 16.
11. "Navigating Trauma—for Teachers and Learners," Harvard Graduate School of Education, April 20, 2022, https://www.gse.harvard.edu/ideas/education-now/22/04/navigating-trauma-teachers-and-learners.
12. Maté with Maté, *The Myth of Normal*, 16.
13. Matthew 5:4; Romans 8:31.
14. Ephesians 1:4-5.
15. Ephesians 1:4-5.
16. Ephesians 1:7.
17. Romans 8:14-15.
18. 1 Corinthians 3:16-17.
19. 2 Corinthians 5:21.
20. Ephesians 1:7.
21. 2 Corinthians 5:17.
22. Ephesians 2:10, NLT.
23. 2 Corinthians 10:3-5.
24. Proverbs 4:23.
25. John 8:32.

CHAPTER 4 | HOPE AT THE WELL

1. John 4:9-10, 13-18.
2. John 4:42.

3. C. S. Lewis to Keith Masson, March 6, 1956, in *The Collected Letters of C. S. Lewis*, vol. 3, *Narnia, Cambridge, and Joy, 1950–1963*, ed. Walter Hooper (HarperCollins, 2007), 758.

CHAPTER 5 | EXPECT TURBULENCE

1. Todd Ackerman, "What to Do When Post-Surgical Scar Tissue Is Affecting You," Houston Methodist, January 26, 2024, https://www.houstonmethodist.org/blog/articles/2024/jan/what-to-do-when-post-surgical-scar-tissue-is-affecting-you.
2. Ackerman, "What to Do."
3. Name was changed to protect her privacy.

CHAPTER 6 | EVIDENCE IS YOUR FRIEND

1. "Radically Transforming Communities," Seed India, accesed December 9, 2025, https://www.seedindia.us/work1.
2. Lorna Collier, "Growth After Trauma: Why Are Some People More Resilient than Others—and Can It Be Taught?," American Psychological Association, November 2016, https://www.apa.org/monitor/2016/11/growth-trauma.
3. Collier, "Growth After Trauma."
4. Ephesians 2:8-9.

CHAPTER 7 | ENGAGE GOD'S GRACE IN THE PAIN

1. "Adolf Hitler: 1889–1924," Spartacus Educational, accessed June 12, 2025, https://spartacus-educational.com/GERhitlerTest.htm.
2. "Biography of Nelson Mandela," Nelson Mandela Foundation, accessed June 12, 2025, https://www.nelsonmandela.org/biography.
3. Nelson Mandela, *Long Walk to Freedom: The Autobiography of Nelson Mandela* (Little, Brown and Company, 2008), foreword.
4. For more on her story, see "Corrie ten Boom," United States Holocaust Memorial Museum, February 10, 2025, https://encyclopedia.ushmm.org/content/en/article/corrie-ten-boom.
5. Corrie ten Boom with Jamie Buckingham, *Tramp for the Lord* (CLC Publications, 1974), 56–57.
6. John 16:33.

CHAPTER 8 | ENTER REST

1. Caroline Leaf, *Cleaning Up Your Mental Mess: 5 Simple, Scientifically Proven Steps to Reduce Anxiety, Stress, and Toxic Thinking* (Baker Books, 2021), 27.

2. Pete Scazzero, *Emotionally Healthy Spirituality*, updated ed. (Zondervan, 2017), 50–53. Scazzero refers to these lies as temptations: "I Am What I Do (Performance)," "I Am What I Have (Possessions)," and "I Am What Others Think (Popularity)."
3. Matthew 4:3.
4. Matthew 4:4.
5. Matthew 4:5-6, author's paraphrase.
6. John 1:46.
7. Matthew 4:7.
8. Matthew 4:8-9.
9. Matthew 4:10.
10. *Up*, directed by Pete Docter and Bob Peterson (Walt Disney Pictures and Pixar Animation Studios, 2009).

CHAPTER 9 | AWAKEN TO WHAT GOD IS DOING

1. Andrea Mathews, "The Adult Who Was Once an Unwanted Child: Healing These Old Wounds," *Psychology Today*, June 10, 2021, https://www.psychologytoday.com/us/blog/traversing-the-inner-terrain/202106/the-adult-who-was-once-an-unwanted-child.
2. Psalm 27:10.
3. Matthew 5:4.
4. Colossians 1:13-14.
5. Romans 7:15.
6. Henri J. M. Nouwen, *Love, Henri: Letters on the Spiritual Life* (Convergent Books, 2016), 24.
7. Psalm 147:3.
8. "Human Trafficking," A21, accessed December 9, 2025, https://www.a21.org/content/human-trafficking/gqe0rc.
9. Christine Caine (@theChristineCaine), "God is able," Facebook, January 30, 2018, https://www.facebook.com/photo.php?fbid=10160063591610089&id=143678730088&set=a.10150570623045089.

CHAPTER 10 | ADDRESS THE HURT

1. 1 John 1:9.
2. Psalm 51:1-2, 17.
3. Berit Ingersoll-Dayton et al., "Unforgiveness, Rumination, and Depressive Symptoms Among Older Adults," *Aging and Mental Health* 14, no. 4 (2010): 439–49, https://doi.org/10.1080/13607860903483136.
4. Ephesians 4:32.

CHAPTER 11 | ADVANCE THROUGH THE SCAR TISSUE

1. Name was changed to protect her privacy.

CHAPTER 12 | ADVOCATE FOR YOURSELF

Epigraph: Years ago I heard this statement. I can't recall from whom.

1. Research suggests it takes an average of sixty-six days to form a new habit. See Jocelyn Solis-Moreira, "How Long Does It Really Take to Form a Habit?," *Scientific American*, January 24, 2024, https://www.scientificamerican.com/article/how-long-does-it-really-take-to-form-a-habit.
2. Name was changed to protect his privacy.

CHAPTER 14 | LEAN INTO LESSONS, NOT LOSSES

1. *Britannica*, "John Newton: English Clergyman and Writer," December 17, 2025, https://www.britannica.com/biography/John-Newton.
2. John Newton, "Amazing Grace," 1779.
3. "John Newton's Tombstone," Grace Gems, accessed July 2, 2025, https://www.gracegems.org/2013/02/Newton.html.
4. "John Newton's Tombstone."
5. Melanie Greenberg, "The Psychology of Regret: Should We Really Aim to Live Our Lives with No Regrets?," *Psychology Today*, May 16, 2012, https://www.psychologytoday.com/us/blog/the-mindful-self-express/201205/the-psychology-of-regret.
6. Greenberg, "The Psychology of Regret."
7. Ephesians 1:7.
8. Ephesians 1:4.
9. Ephesians 1:4.
10. Ephesians 1:4.
11. Ephesians 1:5-6.
12. 2 Corinthians 5:17.
13. Arash Emamzadeh, "Why Some People Will Always Blame Others: Projecting Blame Can Help Regulate Tough Emotions," *Psychology Today*, January 11, 2023, https://www.psychologytoday.com/us/blog/finding-a-new-home/202212/the-surprising-reason-some-people-always-blame-others.
14. "My Way," track 6 on Frank Sinatra, *My Way*, Reprise Records, 1969.

CHAPTER 15 | LET GOD FORGIVE THROUGH YOU

1. Lantie Elisabeth Jorandby, "Forgiveness: Good for Them or Good for You?," *Psychology Today*, October 21, 2024, https://www.psychologytoday.com/us/blog/use-your-brain/202410/forgiveness-good-for-them-or-good-for-you.
2. Jorandby, "Forgiveness."
3. Tommy Cruz, "The Hidden Dangers of Unforgiveness: Physical Side Effects," Freedom Life Coaching, November 22, 2023, https://freedomlifecoaching.org/blogs/life-coach-to-the-rescue/the-hidden

-dangers-of-unforgiveness-physical-side-effects; BetterHelp, "Does Holding a Grudge Hurt You?," updated February 20, 2025, https://www.betterhelp.com/advice/anger/does-holding-a-grudge-hurt-you.

4. Jorandby, "Forgiveness."
5. Matthew 6:14.
6. Matthew 18:22.
7. As described in Jorandby, "Forgiveness."
8. Romans 12:18-21; Ephesians 4:32.
9. Luke 23:34, KJV.
10. Ephesians 4:32.
11. Eshkol Rafaeli et al., "The Self in Schema Therapy," in Michael Kyrios et al., eds., *The Self in Understanding and Treating Psychological Disorders* (Cambridge University Press, 2016), 59–70.
12. Name was changed to protect her privacy.

CHAPTER 16 | BECOME A WOUNDED HEALER

1. Matthew 11:28.
2. Jo Hargreaves (@thefaithfilledtherapist), "Great is thy faithfulness, Lord unto me," Instagram, May 29, 2025, https://www.instagram.com/p/DKQFUgoi-5p.
3. Psalm 77:11-12, NIV.